CONTENTS

'Thoughts are scientific if they correspond to an objective process and make it possible to influence that process and guide it.' – LDB

PLANNERS, POLITICS AND HEALTH SERVICES

GREGORY PARSTON

WITHDRAWN

CROOM HELM LONDON

© 1980 Gregory Parston
Croom Helm Ltd, 2–10 St John's Road, London SW11

British Library Cataloguing in Publication Data

Parston, Gregory
    Planners, politics and health services.
    1. Health planning – Political aspects
    I. Title
    362.1   RA393
    ISBN 0-85664-909-0

TO PETER, ANN AND GORDON

Printed in Great Britain by
Biddles Ltd, Guildford, Surrey

PREFACE

This book documents a phase of my learning. It is not solely about planning or health services or political thought. It does deal with these issues, but, more importantly, it reflects an attempt to understand the *relationship* between what I do as a planner, particularly as a health services planner, and what I think politically.

It is important to acknowledge, from the start, that I have not emerged from this study with any conclusive guide for action. The product of my working and thinking is unfinished; I don't fully understand what the relationship between what I do and what I think is, nor really what it should be.

Peter Medawar (1969) once wrote that four-fifths of his life as a research scientist had been wasted. He meant that the bulk of his work, although, we might add, undoubtedly contributing to the occasional and notable 'scientific achievement', resulted in questions left unanswered, in wrong directions, in blind alleyways from which there seemed to be no return.

The work reported here, insofar as it has attempted to answer questions, falls into my own four-fifths (or more) of time wasted. Instead of answering questions the work has contributed to the realisation that, particularly in fields like planning and health and politics — where, even more than in Medawar's zoology, definitions change rapidly and, with them, personal understanding of their relationships — answers aren't always required. As a result, the ability to perceive, to think about, and to question the kinds of links which exist in one's own mind between thought and action have become much more important to me. I have learned not to accept that planning is a sort of game, where performance can be improved with increased practice and changes in strategy. If planning ever could be compared to a game, my own view is that the only possibility for improvement would come from questioning the purpose and rules of the game itself.

I know that this is not a new thought, that many people, who have thought and worked better and harder than I, have come to the same realisation before. Nonetheless, for me, it is new, and the struggle to answer difficult-to-answer questions regarding thought and action continues.

Paul Streeten, in the Introduction to Gunnar Myrdal's (1962) *Value in Social Theory*, poses 'certain fundamental questions' which Myrdal addressed in his work 'to explore the logical, political and moral foundation of social thought and action':

> Can one be at the same time objective, practical and idealistic? What is the relation between wanting to understand and wanting to change society? How can we free ourselves from thinking in terms possibly appropriate to an earlier age, but no longer appropriate to ours, though still powerful in our intellectual tradition? What are the new presuppositions of social thought which can do justice to the changes in social organization? (p. ix)

The thesis from which this book is drawn was completed in 1977 at University College London, and was my first real attempt to confront these types of questions. It may be important to look at why they arose.

Planning and Health Services

I came to Britain from the United States to study planning, specifically health services planning. My education had been in architecture and economics and, building on these, I thought to gear my research to an analysis of traditional health planning methods. As the research began, I was impressed by the fact that there has not been much work done to further the contributions of existing town planning methods in the provision of health services, and even less done in practice. I wanted to explore this issue further and so my research programme shifted away from a study of planning methodologies to an examination of the interface between planning and health services provision. This involved, among other things, fifteen months of field work, during which I was employed as a health services planner.

Through study and work, two points emerged. First, planning work, whether related to 'towns' or to 'health services', seemed to me to be a process which could be studied as a generic activity. Second, I found that the lack of exchange between those working in town planning and those working in health services planning could be explained partly by the reluctance of those same people to step out of, or to allow others to occupy, their own traditionally defined roles of planners or medics.

Klarman (1976, pp. 10–11), addressing this latter point, throws the blame for the 'traditional insulation of health planning from other kinds of city or urban planning' on city planners who have been reluctant to touch health planning for two reasons. One is the mystique of medicine, the complexity of health care organization and its impenetrability to the intelligent lay person. The second is that city planners are accustomed to dealing with publicly owned and operated facilities.

Klarman's second reason may relate principally to planners in the United States where health services are not, to a large extent, publicly owned and operated. However, the first reason — the mystification of medicine — has become an *international* issue, popular among both the medical profession and some self-professed circles of 'intelligent lay people'. It is discussed not merely as a barrier to the participation of town planners in the provision of health services, but, more importantly, as a barrier to the achievement of effective and efficient health care.

Partly because of the popular appeal of this issue, I felt that it was necessary to look at the broader consequences of 'medical mystification' upon health services planning. This led me to observe that the very popularity of the issue contributed to only a superficial critique. The consequences of medical 'mystification' and associated arguments about 'professionalism' in medicine have been discussed in varying degrees of detail. But few of the popular critics of existing health services provision have extended their analyses beyond the field of medical care to search out underlying causes of these phenomena and to discuss the influence of the causal factors in other social areas. Particularly because my concern was with planning as a *generic activity*, I felt that the scope of study had to be extended beyond the limited definitions of 'the health field' and 'planning' to deal with these social interrelationships.

So, once again, the emphasis of the research shifted, this time to a study of the social context within which the mechanisms for planning the provision of health services operate. Specifically, I was concerned with the social context of my own work — that is, capitalist society. I was attempting to understand more fully, and to establish a basis of social theory from which I could come back to, a more complete and less parochial examination of planning and of health services provision. In this study of social theory arose many of the unanswerable questions which were to form the framework for the bulk of the research.

Influences of Thought on Action

The study of social theory documented here rests in works of political-economics and sociology. In my research, this involved a review of the arguments of planners and health researchers who base analyses of their own disciplines on political-economic and social theoretical foundations.

These arguments, whose ideological bases range from the Galbraithian to the neo-Marxist, raised in my mind the paradoxical question of whether a fuller understanding of the social context of planning contributes to, or detracts from, one's ability to act as a planner. Most influential on this phase of my work was the evolution of my own political thinking during the same period. I began to question whether anything can really be done in health services planning at all, given an unchanging or slowly changing structure of political and economic control — a control which, in its less blatant form, might be seen to throw up defensive barriers like 'medical mystification'.

Many health and social policy research groups are suggesting new directions for the delivery of community health services. They stress themes like increased awareness of individual health needs (e.g., Illich, 1975), prevention of ill-health through a broader understanding of the social conditions which affect health (e.g., Draper, Best and Dennis, 1976), geographic and social redistributions of health services resources (e.g., Klein, 1972), effective and efficient medical cure and care (e.g., Cochrane, 1972), and democracy in health services decision-making (e.g., Knox, 1975). I was led to ask whether these kinds of 'liberalising' proposals really stand a chance of implementation, and, if so, can they be accomplished in the face of political and economic controls which now seem to be preventing their implementation?

If these kinds of changes can only be accomplished at the political-economic level, then, some observers would argue, the planner who advocates them must be prepared to work at that level. But the pragmatist's reply is that the planner who acts politically is risking dismissal from what little position of influence he or she may hold — the concern here not being unemployment necessarily but, rather, complete loss of access to avenues of action. Some more radical observers might say that the kinds of proposals forthcoming from liberal health researchers are only 'playing with the edges' and accomplishing only that which existing power-holders allow them to accomplish. Others, like Navarro (1975), would argue that fundamental changes in the way health services are provided in capitalist countries can only occur after revolutionary political-economic change. Kelman (1975) adds that revolutionary social change will probably result in a change in what people mean by 'health', anyway. If these latter observations are correct — and as a result of my study I have come to think that they are — what is the purpose of proposing health services changes which social redefinition would likely prove historically inappropriate? Are current liberalising studies really only a means by which sanctioning bodies of existing power holders divert attention from more fundamental issues?

These types of research issues looked beyond health services, and, perhaps more intimidating for me, locked in on my own 'professionalism', beyond planning. Can *anything* really be done to change existing discrepancies in the distribution and availability and ownership of social, political and economic rights within a social system which encourages, and even requires, those discrepancies in the first place? Given that the 'system' is controlled by very few, can anything be done within the system without the consent of the few? Certainly, existing power holders will not consent to any move which threatens or undermines their control or power base, so, one might ask if everything which is done *in* the system is necessarily allowed *by* the system for the benefit *of* the system.

These questions are similar to the 'fundamental questions' which influenced Myrdal's work. They are meant to influence thought and action, and they did influence the nature of my study. They are not meant, necessarily, to be answered.

Political Thought

Although I express my political thinking throughout the book, at times in some detail, it will probably make for a clearer understanding of my work if the reader is aware of at least the direction of my thinking from the start.

Most importantly, I reject the notion, still maintained by some positivists, that, like fact and value in science, one can separate personal values from a technically competent performance of one's occupational, and therefore social, role. I hold that the link between social and political attitudes and social actions is an always present relationship, guiding — consciously or not — what one does as a social actor.

Fay (1975, p. 12) has argued this view succinctly:

Men are not generally schizoid in their thought such that they view social life in one way when they wish to study it, and in quite a different way when they come to questions as to how the knowledge they have gained through study or thought is relevant to the practical problems which confront them.

This stand, which finds its roots in classical Western philosophy, in the dialectical arguments of both Hegel and Marx, and at the centre of vociferous debate in the modern social sciences, has not, until recently, been considered explicitly in planning. Instead, technically competent planning has been confusingly equated with value-free neutrality. I reject this equation. Instead I agree with Peter Cowan (1973, p. 5) who argues: 'The opposite of objectivity is bias, not neutrality; the opposite of commitment is neutrality, not objectivity'. In this relationship, commitment (to whatever values) *and* neutrality (which necessarily maintains existing political, economic and social mores) are forms of bias and, therefore, are both value-based. This is an important point in any analysis of planning and it is discussed in greater detail later in the book.

Overall, my political thinking is founded on the view that social action requires political power, the distribution of which correlates positively with the distribution of economic power. In a capitalist economy, which forms the context within which my study has been set, political power is predominantly exercised, directly and indirectly, by those who own privately the overwhelming majority of the productive resources of the society.

Important to this view is a definition of *power*, and here I follow Lukes (1974) who criticises the behavioural focus of traditional definitions like those of Dahl (1961) and of Bachrach and Baratz (1962). Lukes, briefly, focuses on power as decision-making and control over political agenda, which comprise issues and potential issues. This control can occur not only in the presence of actual observable conflict, which the behavioural definitions cite, but also in its absence – that is, in a condition of what Lukes calls 'latent conflict', which consists of a 'contradiction between the interests of those exercising power and the *real interests* of those they exclude'. In my view, it is in this exercise of power that planning is used to control the exposure of social contradictions.

Now, the epistemological bases of the 'interests' and the 'real interests' of which Lukes writes are clearly experiential. In the light of what many social theorists are now writing about re-ordering experiential knowledge to establish new paradigms for social action, I think it is important to consider social actors' perceptions of their own experience and its relationship to society as a whole. Such personal perceptions are not always nor only political or social or economic in character to the perceivers (although I am aware that this may be arguable on the basis of 'false consciousness'). Nonetheless,

these perceptions do guide thinking and, therefore, action. In considering the role of power and interests in analysis of planning activities, then,
although I lean heavily on political-economic relationships, I don't
hesitate to borrow from other behavioural analyses where appropriate
to my argument. This makes for a rather eclectic argument at times,
but one which, I think, stands logically.

I base much of the way I think on my understanding of what
Piaget (1971, p. 9) has called 'operational structuralism'. This is a term
which Piaget uses to describe society as an amalgam of elements wherein
'the logical procedures or natural processes by which the whole is
formed are primary, not the whole, which is consequent on the system's
law of composition, or the elements'.

I make this reference to ontology in order to explain two further
points. First, I regard the relationship *between* the various elements of
society, such as political and legal forms, as primarily economic in
character. That being said, while I accept the primacy of the economic
relationship between the various elements of society, I don't
necessarily adhere to analyses which espouse economic or structural
determinism, particularly when considering the exercise of political
power. Instead, I think that many other, often contradictory,
relationships exist and simultaneously influence social processes and
actions, sometimes sub-consciously, often without an apparent or
directly causal rationale for individual action.

Second, in my view, significant social change is only possible
through the emergence of conflict and, around this conflict — latent
or not — through the exercise of political power. In my view, conflict
is the motive force to social change. Now, I am not under the illusion
that decisions taken in planning, even if they expose or promote
conflict — and that is essentially the purpose I will argue for planners'
work — will in themselves cause, or result in, direct change in the
social power structure. I do think, however, that planning reflects the
'operational structuralism' of society. Because of that, I think that
one's political thinking can be applied to personal action within
planning work to reflect back, in an admittedly limited way, upon the
whole. The central issue here is how a planner whose political thinking
is based on a socialist perspective can work in a capitalist society.

Acknowledgements

There are many people whom I wish to thank, and many more to
whom I must apologise for neglecting to mention them here.

Peter Cowan served as my supervisor in the writing of the thesis which forms the basis for this book. I owe much thanks to him, as a teacher and as a friend.

Gordon Best, Sholom Glouberman, Jonathan Rosenhead, Linda McDowell, Maurice Backett, Steve Merrett, Ann Casebeer, and Bev Nutt read various drafts of the work. Their incisive comments and the time which they took for long, often frustrating discussions, helped me to see what I was doing and what I was trying to do. For the inconsistencies and demerits of the work, none of them can be blamed.

Thanks also to John Cooper, John Weeks, Brian Langslow, Lesley Latter, Marie Giesbrecht, and the Marshall Aid Commemoration Commission for many favours.

INTRODUCTION

This book examines the influence of political thinking upon the role which one assumes as a planner. I attempt to demonstrate that influence by advancing a political view and employing that view to analyse planning work in the provision of health services. My purpose is to ask why planning is as it is. What influences shape the form and substance of planning? What are the values and interests which planners express in their work? Whose interests are they? How are they transformed into planning work?

Part One, *Planners and Politics*, discusses the link between political thinking and planning action. While examining the social context of planning, I argue that social organisation is based on economic elements, the foremost of which is ownership of the means of production. The function of planning as a state activity in capitalist society is discussed and several planning roles which are proposed in planning literature are examined. I criticise these roles as inadequate in the light of the political views which I express.

Part Two, *Planning and Health Services*, examines the planning work of health services planners. Problems which emerge from the health field to affect health services planning are discussed. I delineate what is regarded as the occupational 'action space' of health services planning work and outline the development of the planning process in health services provision. Two cases of planning undertaken in the provision of health services are presented as examples of planners' work.

Part Three, *'Only Connect . . .'*, analyses health services planning from the political view developed in Part One. I discuss the function of health services planning in a capitalist society. In doing so, I argue that the role of planners aids the administrative and legitimatory purposes of capital. The awareness of the determinant influence which political-economy has upon health services planning, as upon other forms of planning, is advanced as the basis for a planning role which recognises the social nature of planning work.

The book does not conclude with any answers, nor with recommendations for planners whose political thinking is sympathetic to my own. There is no guide for action. Instead, the arguments made here are intended to provide a framework for continued thought. Questions which challenge the link between how one thinks and how one acts are only resolved by personal conscience and strength of political commitment.

Part One

PLANNERS AND POLITICS

1 ON PLANNING AND PLANNERS AND THE INFLUENCE OF SOCIAL ORGANISATION

Planning is both an occupation and an idea. As an occupation, planning is work, a job, something at which one labours for a wage; as an idea, planning is a process which is undertaken to meet some desired objective or to fulfil some purpose. For the planner, occupation and idea are inseparable.

Not only planners plan. Each of us tries to arrange beforehand – to plan – many of the events of life. As an occupation, however, planning has taken on a more definite meaning. Many professional planners, irrespective of their particular disciplines, have come to regard planning as 'basically a methodology, a set of procedures applicable to a variety of activities aimed at achieving selected goals by the systematic application of resources in programmed quantities and time sequences designed to alter the projected trends and redirect them toward established objectives' (Robinson, 1972, p. 22).

The word *planning* is often associated with the professional activities of people who plan the provision of urban services and public facilities. The work of town planners, however, is only 'one branch of a family of disciplines and activities which plan and use planning methods, e.g., administration, management, budgeting, engineering and systems analysis' (p. 22). Nonetheless town planning provides a good basis from which to look at other branches of this family of disciplines. Town planning, possibly because of the non-quantifiable nature of many of its goals and objectives, possibly because of its being a relatively older profession than other planning disciplines, has occasioned many practitioners and observers to explicitly address the theory of planning. In so doing, they have provided a large body of writing which can be studied to find the links between occupation and idea. Town planning, too, with its 'public service', physical and spatial orientations, lends itself well as a basis from which to investigate health services planning, particularly in the light of a lack of comparable theoretical discussion and study of health services planning, on the one hand, and of the similarity between health services planning and town planning, on the other. This similarity rests on the nature of the resources with which all physical services planning deals.

Town planning seeks to control or influence the future pattern, or the direction of development, of usually state-financed,[1] and usually urban, services. In most cases, these services are accommodated within, or defined in terms of, physically identifiable elements — e.g., buildings, roads, parks — even though some of the services may possess a greater social than physical value or character. These physical elements require space.

Space is a limited, finite and unique resource.[2] Other types of planning are directed towards the allocation of limited and finite resources. Budgeting, for example, requires the allocation of limited supplies of money. But unlike money or organisation, space, because it implies location, also bears the characteristic of uniqueness. By definition, in geometric terms, each point in space is different from any other. So with urban space. Once urban land, the spatial resource in town planning, is allocated to a particular service or use, that service or use gains the full advantage of its location *vis-a-vis* other physical elements in the city. No other service or use gains that exact advantage. Unlike the allocation of identical amounts of money to different budget areas, there can be no identical allocation of space, as no two spaces can be identical.

Town planning and other forms of physical services planning, then, are seen to deal with the allocation of a limited, finite and unique resource between alternative and possibly competing uses. Land can be allocated to various services, to roads or parks, for example. It can also be allocated within one service, to hospitals or health centres, as another example. But it can only be allocated to one service or sub-service at a time.

Arranging the allocation of this resource is a task of the town planner. Because town planning work entails the formal allocation of a resource which is unique and which is potentially contestable, theoretical considerations of town planning have emphasised its *distributive* nature. Town planners and other planners whose work deals with spatial resources, are seen to face similar occupational responsibilities and to fill similar occupational roles, both of which are, again, distributive.

The way in which an individual fills the planner's role, the personal values and attitudes which the planner brings to working, forms the link between planning as an occupation and planning as an idea. Now, the planner's role is one dimension of *planning action*, a term which I give to planning as an occupation. Planning as an idea gives rise to what I call *planning practice*, a desire or set of desires which provide some purpose for the planner's choosing planning as an occupation. Planning practice, the purpose one has for planning, is directly manifested in the planner's role and reflects the attitudes and values which are formed by the way one views and experiences society. Simply stated, how the planner thinks and how the planner views society, in particular, influence the way the planner works.

Planning Action and Planning Practice

Planning action denotes planning as an occupation, which may be seen to have three dimensions: what the planner plans, what the planner does to plan, and how the planner undertakes planning.

What the planner plans is a pattern of resource allocation. The resources of town planning and other types of physical services planning are primarily spatial in character, whether they be housing, roads or hospitals. Underwood (1976) applies the term *action space* to the range of issues and situations towards which planning is directed, and I will use that term to refer to this dimension of planning action.

What the planner does to plan consists of the several tasks or *operational activities* at which the planner labours. In his reader *Decision-Making in Urban Planning*, Ira Robinson (1972, pp. 27–8) identifies a 'commonly accepted' set of procedures which make up the 'now familiar and well-established model of the rational planning process':

1.   [Goal-Setting] Identify the problem or problems to be solved, the needs to be met, the opportunities to be seized upon, and the goals of the community to be pursued, and translate the broad goals into measurable operational criteria;
2.   [Plan-Formulation] Design alternative solutions or courses of action (plans, policies, programs) to solve the problems and/or fulfill the needs, opportunities or goals, and predict the consequences and effectiveness of each alternative;
3.   [Plan-Evaluation] Compare and evaluate the alternatives with each other and with the predicted consequences of unplanned development, and choose, or help the decision-maker or decision-making body to choose, that alternative whose probable consequences would be preferable;
4.   [Plan-Implementation] Develop a plan of action for effectuating or implementing the alternative selected, including budgets, project schedules, regulatory measures, and the like;

5.   [Plan-Review and Feedback] Maintain the plan on a current and up-to-date basis, based on feedback and review of information to adjust steps 1 through 4 above.

Others (e.g., McLoughlin, Chadwick, Wilson; see Hall, 1975, p. 273) have identified similar sets of procedures, but it is the existence of a *process* itself which is important. Edward Banfield, in his early contributions to planning theory, described planning as 'the process by which he [i.e.: an actor, either individual or organisation] selects a course of action (a set of means) for the attainment of his ends' (1959, p. 139). Similarly, Paul Davidoff and Thomas Reiner, in an often cited paper which offers a framework for planning theory, 'define planning as a process for determining appropriate future action through a sequence of choices' (1962, p. 103). Unlike the activities one undertakes to arrange life's events, the process of the planning occupation is a set of procedures, prescribed by the planner, or by others, which the planner does follow (with greater or lesser adherence) in order to plan.

How the planner undertakes planning is what I have called the *planner's role*. These three dimensions — action space, operational activities and the planner's role — form planning action. How does this differ from planning practice?

Planning practice denotes planning as having some purpose, for the individual, which results from the individual's view of society — that is, from the individual's *socio-political thinking*.

Peter Cowan has described a concept in which the planner's work is seen to take place within the intersection of a planner's individual ideology and an all-encompassing entity which Cowan terms social context.[3] Other theorists have identified constraints which arise from areas external to the planner, from social context, to affect the conduct of planning work.[4] The influencing factor which Cowan identifies is the planner's socio-political view of social context itself.

Planning practice is not an institutional concept. Planning practice connotes praxis, conveying the influence of a planner's socio-political thinking and values upon what he or she does as a planner. Because planning practice is value-based on an individual level, it necessarily influences the attitude, or role, which the same individual assumes in work.

This is where the link between planning action and planning practice, between occupation and idea, occurs. In his philosophical essay on social science, Brian Fay (1975, p. 30) has called this type of link the 'conceptual connection between a view of how one ought to understand social life and a view of how this understanding is to be translated into action'. Two examples may help to clarify the distinction and link between planning action and planning practice.

The Garden Cities

During the late nineteenth and early twentieth centuries, when the occupational activities of town planning were more in the hands of what Cowan has elsewhere called 'practical utopian reformers' (1971, p. 4) than in the hands of professional planners, the operational activities of the planning process were few. Cowan cites three activities proposed by Patrick Geddes in 1915 (see Hall, 1975, p. 65): survey, analysis and plan.

Cowan believes that, in its early form, town planning reflected planners' ideologies predominantly in the operational activity 'plan'. This is perhaps most evident in the work of the garden city planners and their forerunners, and epitomised in the plans of Ebenezer Howard.

The striking characteristics of Howard's Garden City plan (see Howard, 1945) were its 'unity, symmetry, [and] completeness' (quoted in Eden, 1947, p. 137). In order to grasp the ideological context of Howard's work, as reflected in his plan, it is only necessary to look to the sources which Howard himself cited in his book, *Garden Cities of To-Morrow*. Howard saw his scheme as a combination of three distinct sets of ideas: the migrating colonisation proposals of Edward Gibbon Wakefield and of Alfred Marshall, the equality arguments of Herbert Spencer, and the model city plan of James Silk Buckingham.[5]

Marshall seems to have influenced Howard most (Hall, 1975): justifying new town development in terms of minimising marginal social and private cost and distributing labour. Marshall's own political-economic leanings are well-known — Joan Robinson (1973, p. 39) has called Marshall the 'champion of the rentier' — and they provide an ideological backdrop against which the influences on Howard's physical plan can be more closely examined. In this respect, Buckingham's plan for the utopian city of Victoria provided a model from which Howard borrowed heavily.

Buckingham, a radical Christian and a Member of Parliament, believed that the 'great evils of his time [were] intemperance, national prejudice, commercial monopolies, war, competition and the "helpless and hopeless condition of the unfortunate" ' (Eden, p. 129). Like

Spencer, Buckingham took a strong stand against private property rights, which, in Spencer's view, were obstacles to social stability. Buckingham's remedy to these great evils (presented in his book *National Evils and Practical Remedies*) was Victoria, a town which would

> combine within itself every advantage of beauty, security, health-fulness and convenience . . . and which should . . . produce, by the new combinations and discipline under which its code of rules and regulations might place the whole body, the highest degree of health, contentment, morality and enjoyment, yet seen in any existing community. (Eden, p. 124.)

Indeed, Buckingham's model city reflected his purposes directly. Land was to be commonly owned, alcoholic drink and weapons prohibited, even the plan itself specified the residential separation of potentially conflicting classes — all in the interest of achieving the virtues after which Buckingham named Victoria's avenues: Peace, Concord, Fortitude, Charity, Hope, Faith, Justice and Unity.

Almost fifty years later, in 1898, Ebenezer Howard was to use some of these same names for his satellite garden cities. He sought to combine many of Buckingham's physical regulations with Spencer's calls for equity, and with the economic programmes of Marshall and Wakefield, in a manner which would achieve many of their separate advantages. Some of these would be physically tangible; 'pure air and water' and 'high wages', for example. Others were more operational: 'flow of capital' and 'field of enterprise'. Further, by providing a 'third magnet', in the form of a garden city which would attract residents from town and country, Howard saw the opportunity to draw from 'mother earth . . . the source of life of happiness, of wealth, and of power' (quoted in Clapp, 1971, p. 23). The end result would be the most idealistic of Howard's garden city advantages: 'freedom' and 'co-operation'.

With their equidistant placement of amenities and open spaces, their concern for accessibility to transport and communication lines, and their stipulations for common ownership of land, garden cities in Howard's view would provoke a 'social revolution', the result of which would see a

' . . . new sense of freedom and joy . . . pervading the hearts of

the people' . . . Garden cities will establish 'a scientific system of distribution to take the place of chaos, a just system of land tenure for
one representing the selfishness which we hope is passing away . . .'
They will 'silence the harsh voice of anger, and . . . awaken the soft
notes of brotherliness and good will', and will 'place in strong hands
implements of peace and construction, so that implements of war
and destruction may drop uselessly down.' (Eden, pp. 141—2.)

An important reference to Howard's ideology lies in the subtitle of
Garden Cities of To-Morrow: A Peaceful Path to Real Reform. Howard's
development of a 'peaceful path', perhaps mandated by Buckingham's
Christian ideals and Howard's own Quaker associations, provides some
insight into why he employed town planning to seek the source of
happiness, wealth and power, when so many of his contemporaries
were employing more organised political action.

Borrowing from Tolstoy, Howard shed more light on the ideological
purpose behind the garden city plan: ' "All that is needed to break
through the magic circle of social life, deliverance from which seems
so hopeless, is that one man should view life from a Christian stand-
point and begin to frame his own life accordingly, whereupon others
will follow his footsteps" ' (1945, p. 118). Howard's footsteps led to
the garden cities.

The New New Towns

A statement of goals was not viewed in earlier planning efforts as a
necessary activity in the planning process and, although some more
articulate planners, such as Howard, proposed advantages which would
result from a plan in order to justify its implementation, it remained
for the physical plan itself to display planners' ideological intents. As
the planning process changed, so did the influence of the planners'
ideologies.

With the development of systems analysis and cybernetics, and
with the emphasis on decision-making which emerged from post-war
management planning, the operational activities of town planning
have been expanded. Methods originating in other fields have been
incorporated in the town planning process. Monitoring and evaluation
tasks have been developed to provide data which can be used to
modify future actions, and goal-formulation has become an explicit
and formal operational activity. In Cowan's view, it is primarily that
last operational activity which now reflects the planner's
ideological purposes. The British new town movement again

provides a good example of this point, in the form of the Milton Keynes town plan.

No conventional master plan, which would 'detail the ultimate structure of the new city', was produced for Milton Keynes. Instead, non-detailed strategic plans and documentation were intended to serve as 'a starting point . . . for the thinking and planning process which would need to be continued throughout the period of building' (Milton Keynes Development Corporation, 1970, p. 11).

After a brief description of the new town's historical and legislative conditions, *The Plan for Milton Keynes* begins with a statement of goals: 1 — opportunity and freedom of choice; 2 — easy movement and access, good communications; 3 — balance and variety; 4 — an attractive city; 5 — public awareness and participation; and 6 — efficient and imaginative use of resources (pp. 13–18). These goals, which are discussed in great detail in the planners' report, vary according to their physical or operational characteristics. But, clearly, at least part of the ideological purpose which all six goals reflect can be found summarised in the first: opportunity and freedom of choice.

Unlike the case of Howard's plan, there is little literature available from the Milton Keynes planners which helps verify this ideological intent, but there are a few statements, made by the planners during and after their work, which seem to confirm the influence of a belief in 'opportunity and freedom of choice' on the nature of the plan.

After the publication of *The Plan for Milton Keynes*, Richard Llewelyn-Davies, principal of the planning firm which served as consultants to the Milton Keynes Development Corporation, spelled out the influence of the six goals upon the new town plan: 'To provide properly for the future, planners must be prepared for the people's views of life to alter, and they must try to plan the necessary means for those who live in the city to change it, improve it and develop it' (1970, p. 310). So, as choices change, plans must change. John de Monchaux, the planning team's leader and project manager, expanded upon the nature of this influence, saying that the planners 'did not see the city [of Milton Keynes] as a balanced, static situation, but as an instrument for social change'. (MacEwan, 1970, p. 316.)

This concept of 'social change' is reminiscent of the 'social revolution' which Howard foresaw as the result of garden cities development. A few years later, when directing a planning effort for another new town, de Monchaux would state his ideological intent more clearly, seeing his planning effort as the promotion of an 'egalitarian' distribution of opportunity and amenity.[6]

Now, whether or not built cities actually fulfil the ideological purposes of their planners is beside the point. What these examples demonstrate is that 'there seems to come a time when those things which are implicit in the actual behaviour of the designers themselves, begin to operate toward a biased selection of goals and strategies on which to base plans.' (Cowan, n.d., p. 17.)[7] Personal ideology and social context overlap to influence work. Planning action and planning practice are of necessity linked by individual thinking and values.

Perspective and Social Organisation

In rather over-simple terms, the individual takes a look at society, desires something from it or for it, and makes a choice of occupation as one way of getting it. Occupation, then, has some purpose for the individual. Purpose precedes and influences action; action presupposes purpose. The choice of planning as an occupation, then, emerges from the individual's idea of what planning can or might do towards fulfilling purpose and this idea develops largely from the way in which the individual thinks about himself and society and about the relationship between the two.

Now, all of this individual thinking, this development of individual desires and purpose, is what Cowan referred to as ideological context. Individual ideology is often regarded as a set of attitudes and beliefs. But ideology is a social creation, the thinking and views whose formation society influences largely as a result of the way in which society itself is organised and functions. Social relationships within one type of social organisation will influence the individual towards a different set of attitudes and beliefs than would social relationships within a different type of social organisation. So, an individual's attitudes and beliefs are developed *within* social context and the supposed intersection of the ideological and social contexts which influence planning is, in fact, a *union*. Individual ideology, then, as a product of prevalent social organisation, is a condition of a social consciousness which in all social organisations, in part at least, has the effect of perpetuating existing social relations.

Now, this social connotation of the word has led many writers to rather pejoratively identify the use of 'ideology' with 'false consciousness'. This can cause unwanted problems. Mannheim, in his early work, avoided unnecessary argument about social and individual consciousness by substituting the word *perspective* for ideology when speaking about individual thinking. By perspective Mannheim (1968, p. 239) meant the individual's 'whole mode of conceiving things as determined by his historical and social setting'. Perspective is a useful concept here, in that it allows discussion of the way in which purpose and planning present themselves mentally to the individual, without appearing to ignore the relationship between individual and social consciousness which careless use of the word ideology might do.

Perspective, then, is the framework within which one's thinking and desires and purpose develop. Perspective is the mode of conceiving things which influences the individual's actions in different contexts. What an individual thinks about any one thing influences action in different contexts with varying degrees of significance, *vis-à-vis* thoughts about other things.

In town planning action, thoughts about personal income, for example, may influence action more significantly than political beliefs; in other areas or times of action, the reverse may be the case, depending upon circumstances arising from the historical and social setting. Perspective gives rise to thoughts on many things and these thoughts combine in various ways to form purposes relevant to various types of action.

But, perspective doesn't arise out of nothing; perspective isn't a synthetic formulation of an 'intelligible ego'.[8] The way in which the individual thinks, the desires and purposes which the individual forms, and, for the planner, the idea of planning arise from, and are influenced by, social organisation. This is what Cowan referred to as social context, the all-encompassing entity which envelops individual perspective in a union which becomes the 'place' of planning work.

Now, to say that there is an all-encompassing social context is not to deny the various strengths of influences in it. But to consider social context as everything from society's economic formation to the taste of the morning's coffee relegates the influence of the way in which society is organised to that of behavioural or psychological factors. Obviously, such a universal connotation will not do. What is required is an understanding of social context, of society as a whole, which differentiates between factors on the basis of strength of influence which they have on action.

Engels, in an attempt to refute the economic determinist stance of some of his colleagues, offered a differentiating view of the influence of various historical and social elements on society:

According to the materialist conception of history, the *ultimately* determining element in history is the production and reproduction of real life. More than this neither Marx nor I have ever asserted. Hence if somebody twists this into saying that the economic element is the *only* determining one, he transforms that proposition into a meaningless, abstract, senseless phrase. The economic situation is the basis, but the various elements of the super-structure – political forms of the class struggle and its results, to wit: constitutions established by the victorious class after a successful battle, etc., juridical forms, and even the reflexes of all these actual struggles in the brains of the participants, political, juristic, philosophical theories, religious views and their further development into systems of dogmas – also exercise their influence upon the course of the historical struggles and in many cases preponderate in determining their form. There is an interaction of all these elements in which, amid all the endless host of accidents (that is, of things and events whose inner interconnection is so remote or so impossible of proof that we can regard it as non-existent, as negligible), the economic movement finally asserts itself as necessary. Otherwise the application of the theory to any period of history would be easier than the solution of a simple equation of the first degree.

We make our history ourselves, but, in the first place, under very definite assumptions and conditions. Among these the economic ones are ultimately decisive. But the political ones, etc. and indeed even the traditions which haunt human minds also play a part, although not the decisive one. (1968c, p. 682.)

This is a view of society as a whole. Engels separates *elements* of social organisation from remote things and events; the former determine history, the latter are negligible.

Social elements comprise the historical and social settings which determine individual perspective. Together, social elements and individual perspective, the latter being part of society, influence individual action. So, how the planner acts, the planner's role, is derived from purpose which is developed from thinking about and experiencing social organisation. These thoughts are not influenced frivolously, by 'negligible accidents'. As purpose changes with continued thinking and experience, so may the continuing manner in which the planner acts.

The next chapter reviews planners' roles and some of the socio-political thinking which they reflect. In the remainder of this chapter, I will look at some of the more important factors of social organisation which influence how the planner acts. Foremost amongst these is economic organisation; economic context provides, in my view, the principal account of social context. In discussing these factors, I will necessarily expand upon my own view of society, upon my own socio-political thinking, to propose a basis upon which to develop an alternative planning role.

The Influence of the Economic Basis of Society

The formation of a society's economic elements shapes the nature, force and direction of the influences which society, as a whole, exerts on action. In the introduction to *Grundrisse*, Marx (1973, p. 99) analysed the relationship between various economic elements, concluding that while production, distribution, exchange, and consumption form the distinct members of the economic and social totality,

> production, predominates not only over itself . . . but over the other moments as well. The process always returns to production to begin anew. That exchange and consumption cannot be predominant is self-evident. Likewise, distribution as distribution of products; while as distribution of the agents of production it is itself a moment of production. A definite production thus determines a definite consumption, distribution and exchange as well as *definite relations between these different moments.*

So, production, as the predominant member of economic structure, and ownership of the means of production become the predominant influences within economic formation and upon social formation as well.

> In production, men not only act on nature but also on one another. They produce only by co-operating in a certain way and mutually exchanging their activities. In order to produce, they enter into definite connections and relations with one another and only within these social connections and relations does their action on nature, does production, take place . . .
>   *Thus* the social relations within which individuals produce, *the social relations of production, change, are transformed, with the change and development of the material means of production, the productive forces. The relations of production in their totality constitute what are called the social relations, society, and specifically, a society at a definite stage of historical development,* a society with a peculiar, distinctive character. (Marx, 1968, p. 80.)

In a capitalist society, capital, as the means of production, is privately owned. As a result, capital dominates social relations and becomes the 'sum of commodities, of exchange values, [*and*] *of social magnitudes*' (p. 80) because capitalism not only means private ownership of the means of production, but also means private ownership of the means of production *by a portion of society to the exclusion of the other portion of society*. The relationship between the owners of capital and the non-owners of capital (who own only their labour power) is the fundamental characteristic of capitalist society. The lack of capital ownership compels the non-owners to work as wage earners resulting in a 'buying and selling of labour power [which] is the *differentia specifica* of capitalism' (Sweezy, 1970, p. 56). The relationship between those who own capital and those who, not owning capital, must work for a wage

> is the basis for the so-called conflict between Capital and Labour. Actually it is a conflict or struggle of basic interest between two main classes into which capitalist society is divided — broadly speaking between owning capitalists and workers who live by hiring themselves out for a wage. (Dobb, 1958, p. 7.)

Now, the capacity to exercise political power in society correlates positively with ownership of the means of production: 'Such power as may be available naturally and inevitably belongs to capital. Its exercise is the prerogative of ownership ... In the assumption that power belongs as a matter of course to capital, all economists are Marxians' (Galbraith, 1974, p. 65).[9] This is not to say, however, that the power accruing to individual private owners of capital is limitless, even in a strictly financial sense. In varying degrees, the power of individual ownership is restrained by the collective interests of the owners of capital, 'if only in order to give some coherence and stability to the system as a whole' (Dobb, p. 9). One of the ways in which this restraint is exercised is through the formal political and administrative mechanisms of society; the rights and power of capital ownership 'will be bounded by legislation and by the demands of fiscal policy, and "private enterprise" will be subjected in varying degrees to State control'.

The intervening or, at least, interfering role of the state in 'free enterprise' is one characteristic of what has become termed late capitalism.[10] State intervention in the capitalist market-place has arisen in an attempt to compensate for the deficiencies in a smoothly operating competitive free market. Such deficiencies result from a second phenomenon of late capitalism, which is the concentration of economic activity into smaller numbers of multi-national corporations[11] and the expansion of oligopolistic and monopolistic market structures. (See Habermas, 1973.) As the economic power of capitalists grows through simultaneous concentration and expansion, social and economic deficiencies occur, and the self-imposed restraints of the powerful become more formalised and visible in the role of the state. This state role takes its form in what Habermas terms the *legitimatory* system and the *administrative* system of late capitalist society.

The State and Class Struggle

O'Connor's (1973, pp. 6–7) analysis of late capitalist society, which is similar to Habermas's, identifies three sectors within the capitalist economy: competitive, monopoly and state. The state sector 'must try to fulfil two basic and often mutually contradictory functions – accumulation and legitimization'.

Accumulation is promoted through *social capital*, which comprises state investment ('projects and services that increase the productivity of a given amount of labor-power and . . . increase the rate of profit') and state consumption ('projects and services that lower the reproduction cost of labor and . . . increase the rate of profit'). Legitimisation, on the other hand, is sought through *social expenses* ('projects and services which are required to maintain social harmony'). O'Connor emphasises that 'precisely because of the social character of social capital and social expenses, nearly every state expenditure serves these two (or more) purposes [ie, accumulation and legitimisation] simultaneously, so that few outlays can be classified unambiguously'.

The growth of the state functions thus increases in response to the enlarging administrative and legitimatory requirements of the monopoly sector. The supposedly 'public' state socialises capital costs and the social expenses of production while leaving profits to *private* ownership. At the same time the state justifies its own role and legitimises the economic and social formation which necessitate it. Why does this happen?

The state is actually 'the official representative of society as a whole; the gathering of it together into a visible embodiment'. But the state is this 'official representative' only insofar as it is the state of that class which itself represents society as a whole at a given time. (Engels, 1974, p. 73.) In a capitalist society, that representative class comprises the owners of capital.

Engels could not have been clearer about this. Engels and Marx defined 'political power . . . as merely the organized power of one class for oppressing another' (Marx and Engels, 1968, p. 53); Engels later wrote, 'the state is nothing but a machine for the oppression of one class by another' (Engels, 1968a, p. 258). Now, the state is certainly a mechanism through which the capital-owning class organises its political power. But, the exercise of political power in the state is not confined solely to the activities of the capital-owning class. The state also constitutes one arena of class struggle.[12] The working class can and often does organise politically and exercise political power democratically within the state apparatus, even though the state remains the machine through which the capital-owning class organises and exercises officially its power – democratic or not.[13]

However, at the same time that it can extend class struggle, participation of the working class in the state's political arena can foster the interests of the owners of capital. Habermas (1973, p. 368) argues that this is accomplished, and legitimisation enhanced, through formal or parliamentary democracy, where, once the 'loyalty of the masses' is secured, democratic formation of political aims and 'administrative decisions may be taken relatively independently of the aims and motives of the citizens'. By avoiding *real* participatory democracy, owners of capital, whose interests the state represents, attempt to eliminate as a theme of social and political discussion 'the contradiction between administratively socialized production, and a form of acquiring the values produced which remains now as before a private one'.

Now, the political structure of capitalist society derives from the 'Capital-Labour conflict', wherein the struggle between the capital-owning class and the working class takes on a political form. Despite capital's control over social relations, the state and the activities of the state can serve as a forum for class struggle. But where does the power of the working class find its source? Certainly not in capital.

Poulantzas presents a view of power which explains the political form of class struggle. He defines power as *'the capacity of a social class to realize its specific objectives'* (1975, p. 104). Class relations, then, are power relations 'to the extent that the concept of social class shows the effects of the structure of *the relations of the practices of the classes in "conflict"* ' (p. 103). So the source of power rests in the *realisation* of the interests of one class, collectively, against the interests of another, whose values they do not hold in common.

Realisation has a two-fold meaning. It means attainment, and in this sense it deals with the exercise of power; but it also means under-standing — that is, a class's understanding or perception of what its interests are. This second meaning brings with it the concepts of *class-in-itself* and *class-for-itself*.

Both concepts connote common relationships among a particular group of people which arise from that group's particular relationship to society as a whole — a relationship distinct from that of any other group. Class-in-itself, however, comprises people who 'have no tangible or common *interests* which they express' and which would unite them, 'forcing them to act as a unit'. When a class, through social struggle, *realises* its common interest and develops 'a common understanding' of its social relationship, it 'forms itself into a class-for-itself'.[14] In Marx's conception of class power, once the working class has identified its real interests (its 'reality' as opposed to its 'conception' of itself), its power will be cohesive and strong enough to seize control of the constituent elements of social structure. 'Classes-in-themselves [in the meantime] only come to act fully for themselves when they enter the arena of politics, for that is where they experience power [relationships] and open conflict' (Atkinson, 1971, p. 46).

The controlling power of the capital-owning class in a capitalist society derives from its own position in that society (as owners of capital) and from its collective formation of a common interest: simply put, maintaining the fruits of its capital ownership. Its real interests are realised. But this capitalist control makes the working class realisation of its real interest an arduous process. Through its legitimatory and administrative systems, and through its other socially integrative institutions (such as education), the capital-owning class 'will legitimize the *status quo* in countless ways'. The extent to which they succeed, 'both by accident and design, will be a measure of the depth of false-consciousness in the proletariat . . . which involves the acceptance of the authority and rightness of norms, ideas and values which emanate and are internalized from the opposed [capital-owning] class' (p. 47). The power which the working class has, then, is dependent upon how far it has come in collectively forming its own common interests. In the state arena of politics in late capitalist society, that power remains dominated by the structurally stronger power of society's representative class.

The Exercise of Power

In their attack on Dahl's (1961) classical pluralist power model, Bachrach and Baratz (1962, p. 379) proposed a definition of power which includes two 'faces':

> Of course power is exercised when A participates in the making of decisions that affect B. But power is also exercised when A devotes his energies to creating or reinforcing social and political values and institutional practices that limit the scope of the political process to public consideration of only those issues which are comparatively innocuous to A. To the extent that A succeeds in doing this, B is prevented, for all practical purposes, from bringing to the fore any issues that might in their resolution be seriously detrimental to A's set of preferences.

In its 'second face', the exercise of power can prevent issues from entering the political arena altogether. The result, what Bachrach and Baratz called *nondecision-making*, is to exclude from open conflict, and therefore from the power exercises of other groups, issues which A sees as threatening to his position, either in its more open consideration or in its possible resolution in favour of other groups. But like Dahl and other pluralists, Bachrach and Baratz based their definition on the presence of observable conflict, overt or covert. When there is no such conflict, they maintained, it must be presumed that there is consensus between A and B and even nondecision-making is impossible.

Steven Lukes (1974) argues that, while the 'two-dimensional view' of power developed by Bachrach and Baratz is less behaviour-oriented than the pluralist concept, it fails to take account of what he calls *latent conflict*. Lukes sees both the pluralist and the two-face views of power as too individualistic. More importantly, by assuming that the absence of conflict equals genuine consensus, both views 'simply rule out the possibility of false or manipulated consensus by definitional fiat' (p. 24).

In Lukes's 'three-dimensional' view, he defines latent conflict as 'a contradiction between the interests of those exercising power and the *real interests* of those they exclude . . . who may not express or even be conscious of their interests' (p. 25).[15] Power is exercised by one group against another in the form of manipulation, inducement, ideological persuasion. Lukes explains:

A gets (causes) *B* to do or think what he would not otherwise do . . .
But *B* automatically accepts *A*'s reasons, so that one is inclined to
say that it is not *A* but *A*'s reasons or *B*'s acceptance of them, that
is responsible for *B*'s change of course. (p. 33.)

Lukes's definition helps to explain how the administrative and
legitimatory systems of late capitalism are actually exercises of
capitalist power over the working class. Conflicts are made latent
through the manipulatory actions of these systems, with the intent
of improving the conditions under which capital is accumulated. It is
not difficult to see how town planning, as a state activity, can be
employed as an exercise of this third dimension of power.

Town Planning and the State

State intervention in the capitalist economy is intended to compensate
for the dysfunctions of the economic system. Where there is a need to
create and improve 'conditions for the exploitation of surplus
accumulated capital', the state administrative system actually replaces
market mechanisms:

'by increasing national competitive capacity' through the organization of supra-national blocks, imperialistic protection of international stratification, etc;

by unproductive state consumption (armaments and space industry);

by political channelling of capital into sectors neglected by market
autonomy;

by improving the material substructure (traffic, school and public
health systems, recreation centres, *town and regional planning*,
housing construction, occupational training system, further
training and retraining programs etc);

by improving the immaterial substructure (promotion of science,
investment in research and development);

by intensifying the system of social work (educational system);

by meeting the social and material costs attendant on private
production (unemployment benefit, the welfare state, etc).
(Habermas, 1973, p. 367. Emphasis added.)

To Habermas, the place of town planning in economic and social
organisation is unambiguous. But two points must be made to bring

the discussion of the state and economic power to the level of social organisation at which planning work is conducted.

First, consideration of the state can not be divorced from the role of local government which administers town planning activities. Cynthia Cockburn (1977, p. 46) has argued this well:

> Local authorities, including local health, water and transport authorities as well as local education, housing and planning authorities, are aspects of the national state and share its work . . . . [To refer to 'local state'] is to say neither that it is something distinct from 'national state', nor that it alone represents the state locally. It is to indicate that it is part of a whole.

Second, because town planning and other forms of social services planning are undertaken to improve the material substructure of society does not mean that those who do not own capital — the working class — do not benefit from improved schools and health systems and housing. Material benefits which emerge from planning work can be gains for the working class.

> Nonetheless, these services are not *total* gains, because to the state and capital they are not *total* losses. As the working class has an interest in receiving services, so capital has an interest in seeing them serviced. (Cockburn, p. 55.)

Seeing the working class 'serviced' is seeing the reproductive costs of labour reduced. As this results in working class gains, the integration of the administrative and the legitimatory functions of the state becomes crucial and it is here that the influence of economic structure upon town planning action is strongest and most apparent.

Town planning, in Habermas's view of late capitalism, is primarily a capital accumulation activity within the administrative system of the capitalist society itself. But all state-financed activities perform both administrative and legitimatory functions. So, what the planner plans, the action space dimension of planning action, is directed towards the reduction of the reproductive costs of labour and, at the same time, towards the maintenance of the social harmony required for capitalist production.

Economic structure also influences the other two dimensions of planning action, the operational activities of planning work (*what* the planner *does* to plan) and the planner's role (*how* the planner plans).

These influences are not often manifest in formal institutional arrangements, such as the state's administrative and legitimatory systems, but
rather in the *bourgeois ideology* — here I use the word in its social
connotation — which is maintained by the economic structure itself.
Whereas the state apparatus prescribes the particular issues which
town planning is to address — the need for a new shopping district,
say, or for a new town — the economic structure's influence on
what the planner does to meet these issues and its attempts to influence
the planner's continuing attitude toward planning are less overt. These
influences are most often directed through other elements of society,
although they may sometimes be formalised within what Engels called
the various elements of the superstructure (such as the legislative
action requiring regional structure planning in England and Wales, or
judicial action on land use codes in the United States). More important
is the influence which economic structure itself exerts through its
domination of the other elements of society, both material and
ideological. This is primarily reflected in the social relations which
result from economic formation.

Social Relations and the Planning Profession

Within the various sets of social relationships which influence planning
action are the relationships of planners as a group. The social
relationships of planners fall into two categories: the first is the relation
between the profession of planners and society as a whole; the second
is the relation among planners as a collective group.

In his sociological study of *Professions and Power* Terence Johnson
(1972) offers a framework for the consideration of various professions'
social and political power, which is based upon the degree of 'social
distance' between those producing and those consuming goods and
services. Johnson argues that the occupational control and social
status of a particular profession are not derived, as other models
suggest, from an occupational group's progression in some process of
professionalisation, wherein it acquires more attributes or functional
relevance with age and/or organised effort. Rather, the degree of
control which a profession enjoys over its own practice is relative to
the 'social and economic dependence' which consumers of goods and
services have upon the occupational skills of that group for producing
those goods and services. Johnson explains that this dependence
correlates with the collective strengths (i.e., homogeneity) of the
producing and consuming groups, and upon the possible threatening
nature of the relationship (as exists in the 'production' of medical

services, for example).

'Dependence upon the skills of others has the effect of reducing the common area of shared experience and knowledge and increases social distance' (p. 41). Increased social distance creates increases in the uncertainty or tension in the relationship between producer and consumer. It also creates a potential for the producers to impose their own definition of the relationship upon consumers of their goods and services, and thereby resolve uncertainty. Johnson identifies three broad resolutions of uncertainty which exist in producer-consumer relationships. He refers to these as *collegiate control*, *patronage*, and *mediation*, and according to them he categorises professions.

Collegiate control is characterised by professionalism where 'the tensions inherent in the producer-consumer relationship are controlled by means of an institutional framework based upon occupational authority' (p. 51). Two important conditions for this form of control are 'a large and relatively heterogeneous consumer group' and 'a homogeneous occupational community'. The medical profession, in Johnson's view, is the epitome of an occupational group which enjoys collegiate control over the producer-consumer relation.

Oligarchic and corporate patronage is a form of control in which clients, or consumers, have 'the capacity to define their own needs and the manner in which those needs are catered for' (p. 65). Such control is conditioned by 'small, powerful, unitary clientele' and a 'fragmented hierarchical, locally oriented occupational group'. Johnson points out that patronage is characterised 'by practising contexts in which the practitioner must *know* and *do* what is expected of him . . . Practitioners tend to be apolitical, where the expression of political views or political action may embarrass the patron' (pp. 70–2). Accountants and architects are occupational groups which Johnson sees being controlled via patronage systems.

The third type of occupational control, mediation, takes its form from the direct intervention of social institutions in the producer-consumer relationship. The state is the predominant exerciser of mediative control in Johnson's view: 'Mediation arises where the state attempts to remove from the producer or the consumer the authority to determine the content and subjects of practice' (p. 77). Through state intervention the social character of the consumer group is made less important than its unique availability. Under such control, the occupational group tends to be bureaucratised with the result that 'divergent interests and orientation are created within an occupational community' because of the bureaucracy's necessary specialist and hierarchical organisational form. Teachers are an example of an occupational group controlled in this way.

Where do town planners fit? Town planning is a state activity and as such it is professionally controlled, in Johnson's sense of the word, via state mediation. Johnson explains that the extent to which mediative control resolves producer-consumer uncertainty is variable, and indeed, the state may institutionalise its control through the employment of persons in the very occupation it means to control. Now certainly, the state acts as a unitary clientele for planning work and, as a result, planners may be viewed as an occupational group which is controlled via a state patronage system. However, state activity in the producer-consumer relationship, which 'removes from the producer or the consumer the authority to determine the content and subjects of practice', is characteristic of the state's administrative and the legitimatory functions.

The role of the state in late capitalist society leads me to conclude that planners, as an occupational group, are mediatively controlled. But more important than which of these two control systems — patronage or mediation — applies to planners, is the point that in either case the state retains control over the producer-consumer relations of planning work.

A second important social relationship for planning professionals is the relation *among* planners. For the planner, other planners form a 'key reference group' which may have 'a significant influence on the planner's conception of his role' (Underwood, 1976, p. 8). This reference group, which is collectively subject to the same social influences as is the individual planner, can become a means for justifying the role which one assumes as a planner.

The interaction within the professional reference group takes many forms, as do its resulting influences on planning action. One of the important catalysts for this reference group's influence is the common set of values which have been shown to be held by many planners, both on a political level and based on class position (see Marcus, 1971). This underlying cohesion between individuals in the occupational group can tend to subside or reduce possible intra-group conflicts over many of the operational concepts of planning action, even though the various forms which the planner's role can assume do appear to conflict and to reflect quite different political values. How the planner views society is central to all of this cohesion. Planners' views about society influence the attitudes with which the individual planner assumes the work role. This influence is the focus of the next chapter.

Notes

1. O'Connor (1973, p. 10) substitutes the prefix 'state' for 'public':

The conventional phrase 'public finance' reveals the ideological context of orthodox economic thought . . . The phrase 'state finance' is preferable to 'public finance' (and 'state sector' to 'public sector' etc.) precisely because it remains to be investigated how 'public' are the real and financial transcations [sic] that take place in the state sector.

2. I am indebted to Peter Cowan for introducing the notion of space as a unique resource into my argument.

3. This discussion of Cowan's 'Ideological/Social Intersect Concept' stems from a series of lectures which he regularly gives at the Bartlett School of Architecture and Planning.

4. For example, Friend and Jessop (1969) discuss uncertainties arising from the environment, related fields of action, and value judgements; Cassidy (1971) identifies the effects of social indicators, particularly upon evaluation activities; and Goodman (1972) studies the ill-effects of bureaucratisation, professionalism and industrialisation.

5. Eden's (1947) article presents a fine overview of the intellectual climate within which Howard's ideas developed.

6. John de Monchaux, personal communication.

7. Planning for a new town minimises the constraints placed upon a planner's 'biased behaviour' by existing development or regional considerations. Nonetheless, the reflection of planners' ideological purposes, though less obvious, is evident in these 'constrained' contexts. John Jackson's book *The Urban Future* (1972), for example, reviews several regional planning studies to show 'how planners think'. Jackson's analysis deals mostly with planners' operational thoughts *in planning action*, but his section on 'goals and objectives', particularly, provides some insight into planners' more 'subjective' activities in already developed regional settings.

8. This is not to say that an individual's mode of thinking or thinking itself is pre-determined. Habermas argues that to explain 'logical methodological complexes' in terms of empirical or historical causality would either reduce the explanation of technical and practical interest of knowledge to a biological level, or 'realistically deprive self-reflection of the possibility of a justificatory basis for its claim to validity' (1974, pp. 14–15).

9. Galbraith excepts 'professional defenders of the free enterprise system' from 'all economists' of whom he speaks. Among the former he would include Friedman, whom Galbraith quotes as supporting profit maximisation against 'social responsibility' on the part of corporate officials. Corporate social responsibility, in Friedman's view, is one of the few 'trends [which] could so thoroughly undermine the very foundation of our free society' (quoted in Galbraith, 1974, p. 124). For a discussion of how Friedman's teachings in support of 'free enterprise' are 'advancing' free society in Chile since 1973, see Letelier, 1976.

10. The use of the term 'late capitalism' here derives from the work of Mandel (1975) entitled *Late Capitalism*:

The term 'late capitalism' in no way suggests that capitalism has changed in essence, rendering the analytical findings of Marx's *Capital* and Lenin's *Imperialism* out of date . . . The era of late capitalism is not a new epoch of capitalist development. It is merely a further development of the imperialist, monopoly-capitalist epoch (p. 10).

Mandel argues that the roles of the state of monopoly-capitalists and of 'public and private "planning" ' are not capable of neutralising or cancelling the long-term laws of motion of capital described by·Marx.

11. For an analysis of the 'Capital-Labour conflict' in the light of the concentration of economic activity see Braverman's (1974) *Labor and Monopoly Capital.*

12. Indeed, as Atkinson (1971, p. 55) points out, with the passage of the 1848 Ten-hour Bill in England and later universal suffrage legislation in Europe, Engels would come to feel 'that social democracy might allow the working class to vote itself into power . . . "We, the 'revolutionaries', the 'overthrowers' Engels wrote — we are thriving far better on legal methods than on illegal methods . . . The parties of Order . . . are perishing under the legal condition created by themselves".' But the modern connotation of what Atkinson calls 'social democracy' is quite different from that of the nineteenth century German Social-Democratic Party, which Engels saw as 'the decisive "shock force" of the international proletarian army'. (Engels, 1968b, p. 655). Twentieth century 'social democracy' is not democratic socialism.

13. The British House of Lords' actions against parliamentary nationalisation of industries in 1976 is one rather clear example of the capital-owning class's non-democratic exercise of power; the Chilean military's *coup d'état* against Allende's elected socialist government in September 1973 is another, more extreme example.

14. Atkinson (1971, p. 43) discusses Marx's distinction between these phases of class development.

15. Lukes adds: 'Conflict is latent in the sense that it is assumed that there would be a conflict of wants or preferences between those exercising power and those subject to it, were the latter aware of their interests' (p. 25).

2 ON THE SOCIAL THEORY OF PLANNING THEORY

Various elements of society exercise dominating influence over other elements, including thinking and action. Ultimately the determinant influence over the way in which society itself is organised is economic formation. In considering socio-political thinking as it influences planning action, it is necessary to remain aware that society is not only the focus of the individual's socio-political thinking, but also the context from which arise all of the other things about which the individual thinks.

This is an important point. The link between socio-political thought and planning action is not a subsidiary to some other facet of individual thought. Because of the dominant influences of society, socio-political thought ontogenetically precedes planning thought. Planning thought is not primordial. McCallum (1974) is mistaken, in my view, to identify theories of society as a sub-set of planning theory. It is precisely the other way around. And when Healy (1974) writes that planners must search for an ideology (by which she means a 'system' of ideas or concepts) to justify their positions or roles, she is calling for the operation of the already-operative.

The socio-political purposes manifested by planners in their work are a demonstration of the socio-political thinking of the individual under the influence of social context. So, what is sometimes called planning theory — the organised thinking of planners — insofar as it manifests socio-political purpose, is actually a sub-set of thought about society as a whole.

Understanding the Planning Workplace

For the individual worker, the social condition of work is demonstrated in the worker's view of the social result of selling his or her labour: in whose purpose and in whose profit does the workers' work result? (See Phelps-Brown, 1959.)

A person's understanding of the real condition of work, and of all social activity, may be obscured by the ideological legitimatory practices of the capital-owning class and of the state. Whether the understanding of the conditions of work are based on a conscious knowledge of actual social formation or on these legitimatory

47

arguments, they are not value-free.

So, depending upon what his or her values are, or are ideologically affected to be (making the process of thought and choice 'false-conscious'), the worker's attitude can range from identification with, to rejection of, what is perceived as the social result of working. The manifestation of that attitude in the workplace is reflected in the role which the worker assumes while working.[1] In some cases this results in the worker's fulfilling the role which the employer expects the worker to assume; in other cases individual views of society can serve to alter the role which one assumes in work.

As a worker, the planner's socio-political view of the social result of his or her work has a direct influence upon the role assumed in the workplace.

No matter how the individual *perceives* his or her own occupational position, the *reality* of the structural position of planning remains: the town planner sells his or her labour to the state, or to an institutional employer contracted to the state, in a work institution whose structural task is the production of a plan to improve material and ideological conditions for the accumulation of capital. Now, the planner cannot divorce his or her values from the performance of the activities required to undertake that formalised task. So if the planner is to fulfil the role which is prescribed by the state employer, the planner must at least agree, or fail to disagree, with the formalised aims put forward by the state to justify its administering town planning.

However, in a capitalist society town planning and other forms of physical planning are propagandised not as a means to capital accumulation, but rather as the manufacture of a plan for the supply and distribution of some valued product which society needs: housing, roads, hospitals – all in the interest of providing more and better facilities for everybody. The formalised action space of town planning is thus seen to deal broadly with the allocation and distribution of resources. Accordingly, the actual product of planning, a plan, is formally aimed at the achievement of 'stated resource objectives and stated social goals' (Wilson, 1973, p. 26).

Now, the amount of recent literature available on the condition of planning work and on purposes which a planner had *sought* to fulfil in a particular plan is very small.

There has been a good deal of post-planning evaluation to identify to whom the benefits and externalities of a particular plan accrued upon implementation. Case studies of this type often provide a medium for evaluators to voice their values about who *should* benefit from public planning in general — often as a criticism of who does. Meyerson and Banfield's (1955) pioneering effort in Chicago and Dennis's (1970) study in Sunderland are fine examples, both ending in recommendations for greater public participation in planners' work. While many of these studies have provided valuable empirical evidence in attempting to answer 'Who profits?' from planning[2], the evidence does not contribute to understanding the planner's *perception* of who profits from his or her work, nor how that perception influences work.

Planners' views of who profits from their work have become the basis for a normative debate which occupies a substantial portion of what is termed planning theory.[3] The salient questions are more often worded 'What is planning?' and 'What is the planner's role?' rather than semantically related to socio-political thinking and the social result of work. Nevertheless, the discussion does revolve around the issue of planners' attitudes toward town planning work and does reflect the socio-political values of the professional planner and theorist. 'In any consideration of the philosophy and purpose of planning, it is axiomatic that questions of valuation and belief predominate' (Rose, 1974, p. 23).

This chapter attempts to go behind the facade of the various strains of planning theory to identify the social theories which provide their foundations and which thus may be seen to provide the foundation for individual planning action.

Many categories have been applied to the debates in planning theory. None have been satisfactory because arguments which have been presented by supposedly opposing theorists too often overlap, making any clear distinction impossible. I will classify planning theory into three categories: *neutralist, advocate* and *activist*. This is primarily for the sake of exposition. The categories are not meant to accommodate self-contained arguments. Rather, they are intended to identify what seems to me to be a range of arguments which can be explained in terms of three seemingly different views about individual purpose and the formalised aims of planning work.

I shall argue, however, that the range of mainstream planning theory is based largely on an acceptance of the formalised and propagandised relationship between planning work and resource-distribution. The distribution component of planning work, emphasised by the unique and competitive nature of its spatial resource, serves as the principal current of planning theory. This results in what I see as nearly a complete theoretical disregard for the part which planning plays in production, the predominant moment of social organisation.

The Neutralist View

The neutralist position is based on the contention that the purpose of planning, as formalised in the expressed aims of the state, is proper. This propriety is derived either from a value-based agreement with the perceived social result of planning work or from the belief that the planner should not question the formal aims which have been determined through an assumed democratic exercise of political power. In either case, the neutral planner should work expertly and efficiently, not only to achieve pre-determined social results, but also to not interfere with them. In the neutralist view, the planner's role is often regarded as one of a technician, manifest in two ways: by *remaining* neutral and by *ensuring* neutrality.

Walker and 'The Planning Function in Urban Government'

The modern — i.e., post-World War — beginnings of the neutralist view that the town planner must remain neutral to political decision are found in Robert A. Walker's (1950) argument, first published in 1941, that public planning should be a staff-function of local government. Regarded at the time as a definitive attack on what Walker saw as the incompetence, amateurism and partisanship of American planning commissions, *The Planning Function in Urban Government* likened the appropriate role of planners to that of a military staff 'whose function it is to assist and advise the commanding officer but not to command in its own right' (p. 171).

Citing the need for a continuing, full-time city planning agency, Walker identified the planning staff's operation as one of research, advice and co-ordination for the executive office of local government. Its service is directed toward the executive office only; its job is 'not to propagandize either administrative organization or the public' (p. 172). Walker suggested ways for insuring the planning staff against political dismissal and for removing the planning function from the realm of politics where citizen planning commissions had met their doom. It is for the politician, who is properly influenced by public pressure, to decide which alternative presented by the planning staff best meets those pressures. 'The final decision as to specific policies must rest with elected representatives' (p. 175).

Walker saw the purpose of public planning as gaining 'maximum returns in terms of public welfare' (p. 110). By determining goals and devising patterns to achieve them, public planning, in the neutralist view, is a means for making the 'urban community a more satisfactory place for humans to live and work in' (p. 362). Walker did not feel, however, that the goals of particular planning projects as determined by the politician are always appropriate. Indeed, 'the usual channels of public information and the political process as it is normally carried on are completely inadequate in the issues of the day' (p. 366).

Given this inadequacy, there exist three alternative roles which are available for town planners and planning agencies: (1) to advocate 'such lines of future development as they think best', (2) to attend 'to problems of relatively slight social or political consequence', or (3) to serve 'as confidential advisors and assistants to incumbent officials, letting such parts of their recommendations as may appeal to these officials become part of the latter's own policy and program'. If planning staffs — whose activities, Walker was quick to point out, depend upon the budget process — venture 'into the political arena, and risk the vicissitudes of all who enter there', they jeopardise their existence. The first role, then, must be avoided. The second role had contributed to the failure of contemporary planning agencies and commissions, and Walker saw no benefit in assuming it again. In Walker's view, the third role 'seems to be the only tenable one' in the long run (pp. 366–7).

As to the question of 'What can be done if public officials refuse to assume the responsibility for community planning or if plans proposed are incompetent' the answer rests 'in an alert and informed citizenry' (p. 369). Alert it may be, but Walker avoided saying how citizens will be informed with all public planning staffs' reports communicated only to the same public officials and made public only with their approval (p. 172).

Neutrality and the Public Interest

Social and political forces since 1950 have tended to shift the emphasis of the neutralist arguments first posited by Walker, especially those limiting the participatory role of public groups in planning. Nonetheless, the neutralist view remains widely held in varying revisions of Walker's stance, the most entrenched of which argues that the planner must ensure neutrality in the name of the 'public interest'. But now, as before, the neutralist view maintains that the planner and the politician play different and necessarily separate social roles.

Shortly after Walker's influential second edition, many students of town planning were characterising the planner's role in such sociological jargon as 'predominantly universalistic, affectively neutral, collectively-oriented and functionally specific as well as achievement oriented'. This role was interpreted as one of a full-time professional in a field marked by technical standards of achievement for the evaluation of performance; who operates in the absence of conventional profit motives, with the presumption that he will be sparing in the intrusion of his values and will venerate 'objectivity'. (Dyckman, 1961, p. 165.)

Objectivity, in this interpretation, seems to be the mechanism by which planners recognise an entity termed 'public welfare' or 'public interest' as the prime determinant in the distribution of planning's social benefits. The neutrality argument gained strength — and at the same time earned its attack — on this very point.

The 'Great Debate' of the early 1940s concerning the issues of an 'open' (capitalist) society, freedom and the nature of public good — argued inconclusively by Hayek, Popper and Wooton (Friedmann and Hudson, 1974) — was overshadowed in the planning theory of the 1950s and early 1960s by the neutralist view that there is little scope for planners in determining the public interest. The growing conflict between the planner and the politician as to which should serve the public in 'providing leadership in achieving the good life', wrote Beckman (1964, p. 324), 'can best be resolved, and the planner's effectiveness enhanced if he is willing to accept the vital but more limited role that our system assigns to the public employee [i.e.,] assisting and serving the elected policy-maker'.[4]

Glass (1959) and others regarded that same 'system', however, as promoting 'a vested interest in the maintenance of the *status quo*' (p. 62). With this view, she argued that the planner's role must *ensure* neutrality in pursuing, rationally and justly, the public interest. This pursuit, said Glass, is the *raison d'etre* of planning which is liable to be subverted by 'arbitrary administrative decisions [which] follow from arbitrary value judgements'. This argument expands the neutrality stance of Walker and adds a second dimension to the planner's technical role. The socio-political purpose of the planner's work becomes the achievement of public welfare, the satisfaction of the 'public's interest', by making sure that *no one's* personal values interfere with its pursuit — neither the planner's nor anyone else's.

Recently there have been attempts to develop this proposed role for the planner in technique, most importantly in the work of Russell Ackoff. Ackoff (1974b, p. 366) seeks to replace the commitment to client organisation, which often characterises the work of planning 'professionals' (among others), with a 'love for all' — that is, for client- 'participants' *and* for all 'stakeholders' who are affected by particular decisions. 'Loyalty to one [interest]' is the virtue of 'a servant', argues Ackoff. A professional, on the other hand, 'seeks to serve his client as well as possible but in doing so seeks to serve all others affected by his service.'[5]

Ackoff bases his case on the belief that

> the principal task of the manager and the management scientist is to learn how to remove the apparent conflict between these levels of purpose – subsystem [the parts and people of, or affected by, a client-organization], system [the client-organisation], and suprasystem [society] – and to find strategies which serve each of them efficiently. (p. 362.)

With the purpose of operationalising that task, Ackoff (1976, p. 300) developed an 'interactive', 'idealized future', participative planning method which involves 'the idealized redesign of a system' free of financial and political constraint while, at the same time, viable enough to provide workable guidelines for desired development. Such idealised planning – and Ackoff proposes that his method could be applied to plan new systems of education, health, transport, and development, and in response to problems of crime, race, generation gaps, and litter (1974a) – 'forces those involved to rethink each aspect of life' and allows them to improve their own quality of life with a regard for the scientific (which Ackoff labels 'the pursuit of *truth*'), the political-economic ('the pursuit of *plenty*'), the ethical-moral ('the pursuit of *goodness*'), and the too-often-'ignored' aesthetic ('the pursuit of *beauty*').

Ackoff's concern is the democratic resolution of social conflicts. In the face of critics who argue that he does not recognise the structural character of conflict or its power relationship (Chesterton *et al.*, 1975), Ackoff (1975, p. 97) rebuts:

> I propose a *circular* organizational design which is directed as a democratic distribution of power among all levels of an organization ... But my critics base their argument on the assumption that in an asymmetry-of-power situation those with less power have little, or no responsibility to the whole ... The goodness or badness of power is not a matter of whose hands it is in but of how it is used. Power can corrupt a majority as well as a minority as it has often done so ... What is not obvious to me is that there is *any* subgroup of society (no matter how large) in whose hands absolute power can

be placed with absolutely no cause for concern.

Ackoff's belief that inter-group conflicts are resolvable clearly pre-supposes that a common purpose exists and can be identified within his definition of 'subsystem-system-suprasystem' relationships.[6]

Such relationships, in Ackoff's view, rarely include exploitive or abusive behaviour on the part of any organisational components, and even when conflicts do arise in those rare cases, they can often be resolved by changing the behaviour and desired ends or purposes (of which party — exploiter or the exploited — Ackoff does not say). 'Most conflict that appears to be unresolvable at one level of means or ends is subject to resolution at a higher level of desirability' (p. 96). It is thus the role of the planner of social systems to identify the common level of desirability, the common interest, toward which all members of social organisation can strive.

The difficulty in fulfilling this role of ensuring neutrality — or, more accurately, neutral balance — rests on the unaddressed and un-resolved problem of ascertaining the real interests of the various 'parts' of a social organisation. It also begs the question of whether or not the public's common interest, which is influenced and defined and voiced through the legitimatory mechanisms of those who dominate the 'asymmetry-of-power situation', lies in maintaining the *status quo* anyway.

The Neutral Planner

Despite these counter-arguments, many planning theorists have rallied around the idea of a 'neutral pursuit of the public interest' as the planner's purpose. 'Rationality' and 'comprehensiveness' have become the catchwords of the neutral planner's work (see Banfield, 1959). In the neutralist view, planning remains 'the application of scientific method — however crude — to policy making. What this means is that conscious efforts are made to increase the validity of policies in terms of the present and anticipated future of the environment. What this does not mean,' asserts Faludi (1973, p. 1), 'is that planners take over in the field of politics.'

Few town planners want to take over politics, but for those who see the political role of 'advocating particular lines of policy' (Walker, 1950, p. 366) as the only way to pursue the public interest, Gutch (1970) offers a warning of the consequences of drifting away from neutrality. In Gutch's view, political action in planning should be directed toward protecting the interest of the community. But to do this the planner 'either makes an implicit value judgement or runs the risk of conflict with the politician'. Seeming to agree with Beckman's view that the politician always wins in such conflicts, Gutch rules out political conflict as a part of planning work; value judgements, however, can be introduced as an alternative to engaging in political conflict. This latter point seems to be a big departure from the neutralist stance, but Gutch carefully limits the influence of the planner's values to matters relating to technical skills. Where judgements concern 'how many alternative plans he should evaluate', for example, the planner has a wide scope of value-influenced choice, but 'when he has to decide how to weigh the different goals of the different sectors of a community . . . the planner should hand over to the politician' (p. 391).

Now, the neutralist argument does not contend that *town planning* is divorced from political or value-based activity. Indeed, 'planning must take account of political goals', write Rapkin and Ponte (1975, p. 26). But *planners* must recognise that they are not politicians and 'that whatever policy is chosen will benefit some groups at the expense of others. The delicate compromises required to maintain an equilibrium between contending groups call for experienced political judgements, which typically occur among decision-makers at the highest level. Planning should be viewed as a guide to these decision-makers', a guide to others' political activities (p. 27).

It is in this guiding action that the planner must remain neutral and ensure neutrality. The participation of social groups in planning can be one method of doing this. Indeed, in Ackoff's view, participatory planning is a means by which the planner maintains his objectivity. In order to make this argument, Ackoff (1974b, p. 370) has gone so far as to redefine 'objectivity' in keeping with his participative design methods and seemingly align objectivity with some notion of commonly attained interest:

> Objectivity is not the absence of values in purposeful behaviours, simply because purposeful behaviour cannot be value-free. Objectivity is the open interaction of a wide variety of individual subjectivities: it is a systemic property of science taken as a whole.

McLoughlin's (1970, p. 86) picture of the physical planner as a 'helmsman steering the city' down a course charted by society — presumably in 'open interaction' — seems the appropriate role for the planner in the neutralist view: making sure the city's ship does not run aground, maintaining and assisting the commanding political officers, and knowing — and fearing the fact — that the planner is expendable.

The contemporary stance of neutralist planners may be summarised as viewing the social purpose of town planning as the pursuit of the common public interest. The procedures by which the public interest is ascertained remain unclear. However, in the neutralist view, the political process — regarded as something distinct and independent of the planner's work process — affords the public the opportunity to represent whatever its interest is via elected officials. As sole interpreters of the public interest, then, *politicians* maintain sole responsibility for drawing up the contracts for planning work. The planner's attitude toward work and his or her manifestation of that attitude in the workplace should be characterised by a rational and just pursuit of the public interest, accepting 'rationality', 'justice', and 'public interest' as defined politically by actions other than the planner's.

On the other hand, the planner must ensure objectivity, however defined. Fay (1975, p. 28) has referred to this type of stance as the 'sublimination of politics', where politics results in the values of any one social group clashing incompatibly, irreconcilably and irrationally with 'objective answers established through the rational use of evidence and technique'. Just as 'science provides the paradigm example of proper thinking' for the objectivist view of social science, so, for neutralist planners, technical competence and rational comprehensive methodology link the operational activities of town planning work to the planner's role.

The Advocate View

A second view of the purpose and social results of town planning work has been presented most influentially by Paul Davidoff (1965) in an article entitled 'Advocacy and Pluralism in Planning'. This view espouses a role in which the planner serves as a direct advocate for the interests of a community group which is competing with other groups for the benefits of community development. The planner is no longer isolated from political activity; the planner makes political choices in a pluralist arena.

Davidoff's article made popular the word 'advocacy'. Other theorists, however, had done the groundwork in the development of the advocacy stance. Most articulate of these has been Melvin Webber.

Egalitarian Planning

Webber (1963, p. 233) openly voiced the questions of many planners who were, and are, troubled by the neutralist role: 'What are our purposes? In what ways can we, who hold such responsibilities for the physical city, so conduct our affairs to positively affect the lives of its residents?' In response, Webber suggested that the planner's role comprises three responsibilities.

The first responsibility of the planner is to 'extend access to opportunity'. This responsibility is aimed at improving the rationality component of planning work, a component which remains widely accepted in spite of its neutralist foundation. In Webber's formulation, the planner must work 'to help assure *one* that the distribution of the benefits among the city's publics is consciously intended and democratically warranted, *two*, that levels and priorities of investments are so staged as to induce the desired repercussions in the private markets, and *three*, that public resources are used for those projects and programs promising the highest social payoffs.' (p. 233.)

An important notion in this first responsibility is that of 'publics'. This was not a new concept; its basis in planning theory goes back to the arguments of Hayek and Popper and it is supported by the social science studies of Dahl and Lindblom (1953). Nonetheless, it threw a strong counter-punch at the neutralist planners' idea of a comprehensible and unitary 'public interest'. The notion of a plural public implied that the social benefits of planning work are somehow distributed among different and competing social groups (though they may not necessarily compete for the same type of benefits). This was to form an important concern in the development of the advocacy perspective.

Webber's second responsibility for the planner is to 'integrate larger wholes'. Here he repeated a traditional definition of planners as 'artist-scientists' who, as 'custodians of the holistic view and the utopian tradition', gain their highest respect when they raise civic aspirations and force solutions to be sought within longer-term policy frameworks. (p. 238.)

Third, the planner's role encompasses a responsibility to 'expand freedom in a pluralist society'. Citing a number of guiding principles in this quest for expansion of freedom, Webber argued that the planner must work to find 'those wealth increasing approaches in setting municipal-investment priorities that will benefit *all* members of the society' (p. 241). Warning that 'it is too easy either to invoke the doctrine of majority rule in usurping individual rights or to invoke the doctrine of individual rights in limiting majority freedom' (p. 239), Webber introduced the notion of egalitarianism in planning, a notion upon which advocacy supporters made their stand.

Plural Planning

The planning workplace in the emerging advocacy view was seen as the market-place. It still is. In 1957 Handler had argued for a theory of planning based on (capitalist) economic theory. 'Planning of any kind is possible only when a surplus exists,' said Handler (1957, p. 147), and the chief problem of planning is to choose the kind of capital into which surplus should be transformed.[7] These choices comprise the goals of planning.

Much of the subsequent discussion in planning literature centred around the problem of choosing goals and the methods most appropriate for their achievement (see particularly Banfield, 1959; Lindblom, 1959; Davidoff and Reiner, 1962; and Dror, 1963). Although developments in planning theory did not adhere to an economic framework as Handler had wished, parallels were drawn between the difficulties associated with choice of planning goals and those faced in 'free market' economic behaviour.

In the capitalist market-place many interests are represented, each registering competitive claims for market surplus. Similarly, in the planning market-place many interests voice claims for the benefits of plans. These interests were seen to coincide with Webber's 'publics'.

Adam Smith had argued that competing self-interests were the basis for the successful operation of the 'free' market economy, for the production of profit — self-interests, that is, aided by the mystical, equilibriating 'invisible hand'. With *The End of Laissez Faire* and *General Theory*, Keynes had demystified the 'invisible hand', suggesting ways in which he believed market intervention could help to make all self-interests more competitive. Just as Keynesians argued that the less powerful voices within a capitalist economy require the aid of public intervention to at least be heard, so a new group of planners began to argue that less powerful voices in the planning market-place require assistance to register claims on 'municipal-investment priorities'. Many planners, whose own perceptions of the social results of their work had led them to become frustrated with the neutralist stance, saw a new alternative.

The planner could work as the invisible or 'hidden' hand in the planning market-place (Halsey, in Dennis, 1970, p. 21). The planner could act politically by representing directly the views of competing publics, thereby seeking the benefit of all members of society, not just those whose voices are powerful enough to claim more than their 'just' share of the goods of planning. Planners began to consider 'market aid or replacement' (Davidoff and Reiner, 1962) as one of the principal functions of planning. Planning analyses became crowded with economic vocabulary and techniques: utility and preference curves and Pareto optimality led the way.

Davidoff's (1965) article on advocacy and pluralism jelled these arguments. Calling for what he labelled 'plural planning', Davidoff maintained that the 'unitary planning' of centralised community planning agencies had discouraged full citizen participation. The interests 'both of government and of such other groups, organizations, or individuals who are concerned with proposing policies for the future development of the community' must be represented by planners directly in the town planning process if 'an effective urban democracy, one in which citizens may be able to play an active role in the process of deciding public policy,' is to be established (p. 332). The 'adversary nature of plural planning' would help provoke lively political disputes which 'could do much to improve the level of rationality in the process of preparing the public plan'.

The role of the planner in this view is one of an advocate for the interests of a group 'with whom he shared [sic] common views about desired social conditions and the means toward them', a group which holds 'values close to his own' (p. 333). The planner, whose responsibility is to represent and plead the case of the client, works to gain that share of the benefits of planning which the client group deems proper. 'The advocate planner would be more than a provider of information, an analyst of current trends, a simulator of future conditions, and a detailer of means. In addition to carrying out these necessary parts of planning, he would be a *proponent* of specific substantive issues.' (p. 333.)

The product of the advocate planner's work, then, 'is the embodiment of particular group interests' (Peattie, 1968, p. 81). But recognition of the wider nature of planning work being at the same time adversary and pluralistic is equally important. Any public, 'any group which has interests at stake in the planning process should have those interests articulated.'

The social theory underlying this stance is, clearly, the political pluralism embraced and supported by such scholars as Dewey, Dahl and Durkheim:

In essence, political pluralism conceptualizes the process of decision making as a system of social relationships whereby the expression of power among and between competing group interests ultimately shapes the direction and structure of the social system. (Mazziotti, 1974, p. 40.)

Davidoff argued that there are many advantages to plural planning in what he viewed as a pluralist society. Plural planning

> would serve as a means of better informing the public of the alternative choices open . . . It would improve planning practice by . . . forcing the public agency to compete with other planning groups to win political support . . . It would force those who have been critical of 'establishment' plans to produce superior plans, rather than only to carry out the very essential obligation of criticizing plans deemed improper. (pp. 332–3.)

The role of the advocate planner in this scenario is one of stirring lively political debate to help inform the competing interest group, with whose values the planner agrees, and of pleading the group's case in a manner similar to a legal advocate; but like the legal advocate, the advocate planner must submit to a decision from some higher political authority.

In this case, Davidoff saw decisions regarding future courses of action for the community as still 'the obligation of the public planning agency' (p. 332). Davidoff granted that in the past these decisions were taken on 'incomplete and shallow analysis of potential directions', but plural planning would help overcome this deficiency and would 'do much to improve the level of rationality in the process'.[8]

The Advocate Planner

Although Davidoff urged planners to engage in the political process, his rules for advocacy offer the planner little more than Walker's second of three alternative roles: to attend 'to problems of relatively slight social or political consequence'. What Davidoff seems to have been looking for in proposing the advocacy alternative is a loyal opposition which accepts that 'proper policy is that which the decision-making unit declares to be proper' (p. 335). Davidoff had seen the possibility of party political advocate planners, in which case public planning agencies would have 'majority' and 'minority' staffs. However, the practicalities of organisation and finance meant that advocacy planning would be centred more likely around *ad hoc* protest associations which would look to government grants for financial assistance, if not for financial existence.

The contemporary stance of advocate planners remains rooted in the concept of egalitarian planning. It is aimed at what Stewart (1973, p. 219) has identified as 'the problems surrounding the demand for and supply of goods (both in the private and the public sector) and thus at the market (or extra-market) forces likely to influence the allocation and distribution of resources within and between communities'. The planner becomes the direct representative of one (or more) of the many interest-groups or publics which compete in the market for shares of the benefits of town planning.

An important characteristic of the advocate's role is its duality, comprising both immediate and longer term purposes. The immediate purpose of the advocate planner's work is identical with that of the group which he or she represents. The benefits gained accrue to the group. But the egalitarian concept of the advocate view also assumes, if not demands, that *all* of the city's publics will or can be assisted and advised by advocate planners. The resulting 'free market' competition between various groups to win political support for their respective plans will produce a more effective, more rational and more democratic plan for all groups concerned. Thus, a broader, longer term purpose of advocacy planning results from the combined influence of various competing advocacy efforts, each seeking its own immediate benefit. This synergic benefit is the 'allocation of scarce resources to different groups in a constrained spatial context based on an understanding of the role of individual and group preferences, and market forces within the overall context of a mixed economy' (Stewart, 1973, p. 205). The longer term purpose of advocacy planning, then, is the egalitarian distribution of the perceived benefits of town planning within a market place whose assumed freedom and egalitarianism is protected by advocacy itself.

Neutralists and advocates differ significantly in the extent to which they support the planner's manifesting personal values in the workplace. Neutralists argue that the planner must not act politically, must not enter into direct conflict with the politician. Advocates, on the other hand, argue that the planner can act politically, can make political choices, and can work to represent a particular political view, so long as the actions of competing planners are subsumed within a pluralist balancing act, controlled by some higher political authority, which achieves the common good. Both the neutralist planner and the advocate planner, then, despite differences in immediate objective, work toward what they see as the common interest.

The Activist View

Of the views categorised in this review, those which I term activist are
the most recently recognised in town planning theory. The relative
modernity of the activist view and its appeal, especially to those planners
who have found advocacy to be frustrating, elitist or patronising, has
contributed to its current popularity as a debating topic. This newness,
however, means that the activist argument is also the least unified and
perhaps the most contentious of the three views.

For many advocate planners it became difficult to ascertain where
lay political action stopped and where the role of the politician began.
As a result of the difficulties which have been encountered in trying to
work as an advocate without direct political recognition (see Peattie,
1968), some planners began to favour a planning role which breaches
the politician's traditional domain. Many reasons are cited in support
of this argument, most of them based on claims of practicality and
realism. Reasoning that planners already possess many of the skills of a
politician, Rabinovitz (1967, p. 267) neatly summarised this view.
'Only if the profession's image includes the picture of the planner as
rightfully a political actor', she wrote, 'will the planner attain both
professional rewards and completion of concrete programs'.

As a consequence of arguments like Rabinovitz's, many theorists
moved away from the advocate camp and began calling for a new
professional position in which planners would exercise some of the
skills of the politician, especially those required to 'marshal effective
influence' in support of planned action (p. 271). Some planners, then,
would maintain their dominant position in 'technical competence,
client relations, rules concerning advertising and actions in the
community', while others 'would specialize for the political role of
opinion-moulding' (Faludi, 1973, p. 236). Other theorists argued that
the planner must assume, *in addition* to technical labels, the mantle of
diplomat or political negotiator (Fagence, 1975), or must learn the
additional cognitive skills of a public policy analyst (Rondinelli, 1973).[9]

Support of direct political activity on the part of the planner does
not characterise planning theorists as activists. Planning theorists who
adhere to the advocate lines of egalitarianism and pluralism see the
planner as a key actor in the political processes which effect decision-
making. Yet the advocates, in supporting political activity in planning
work, regard its purpose as a type of 'mutual adjustment process'
(Warren, 1969); the equilibriating force of pluralism must always
prevail. This is the foundation argument of advocacy.

The activist view builds on the notion of a direct political role for the planner, but the activists reject the advocates' assumption of an egalitarian ethic. This is the crucial difference between the two views.

Rejection of the 'Equal Share' Principle

The activist case is based on the socio-political view of economic and political power as not being held in equal or competitive shares by all social groups, nor in a manner which would result in some sort of Pareto optimal distribution of the benefits of planning, in some sort of common interest. In the activist view, economic and political power determine the distribution of town planning's benefits and planners who attempt to be neutral or egalitarian only complement and reflect that power structure. (Davies, 1972.) Consequently, regardless of whose benefit is intended in the planner's immediate aims, existing planning roles will inevitably result in dominant power holders' benefit and profit. In the event, those who currently hold controlling power in the market will employ that power to retain their current share of existing resources and to obtain at least similarly proportioned shares of any new resources. In the activist view, this ultimate phenomenon thwarts any immediate purpose which can be manifest in planning work.

Unlike the neutralist and advocate role, the activist's role is a manifestation of a perceived conflict between the social results toward which the planner wishes to work and those which the planner sees as being fulfilled in fact. The activist planner rejects the concept of egalitarianism. The activist argues that because the political-economic market is not a truly egalitarian system, any action which supports market mechanisms, in a purported attempt to maintain equal opportunities for all social groups, can only further strengthen the position of the already-powerful.

Harvey (1973, p. 74) voiced this argument, saying that in theory a balance distribution of public services and externalities 'will only happen if the political process is so organized that it facilitates "equality in bargaining" between different but internally homogeneous interest groups'. In practice, however,

> considerable imbalance exists in the outcome of within- and between-group bargaining over external benefits and costs and collective goods because (1) different groups have different resources with which to bargain, (2) large groups in the population are generally weaker and more incoherent than small groups; and (3) some groups are kept away from negotiations altogether.

Harvey (in his then admittedly 'liberal' view) saw the need for a new planning approach which recognises 'the necessity for the redistribution of power, broader access to resources, and expansion of individual choice to those who have been consistently denied' (Sherrard, 1968, p. 10, quoted in Harvey, p. 9).

This recognition is the crux of the activist argument. If what Harvey terms 'social justice' is to be achieved, the planner's work must be directed toward enhancing the benefits of the historically deprived. However, groups whose current holding of power, resources and choice are too weak to make a substantial claim on the perceived benefits of planning will not gain strength from the additional assistance of planners' work if this assistance is also available to those whose power, resources and choice are strong enough to dictate distribution.[10] The activist planners' role involves *taking sides to the repudiation of existing dominant power holders* whose interest is the continued political and economic oppression and exploitation of the weak. Taking sides *in this way* is an overtly political act and the activist planner thus becomes a political actor assuming the role of a politician.

Planning and Politics in Practice

The activist argument is not unique to town planning work. It is a growing view of the conditions of many types of work, a view which argues the mingling of traditionally defined occupational roles with roles traditionally identified with the politician. The arguments of the activist planners — even more than in the cases of neutralist and advocate arguments — do not present a unified view. Yet, while seeming to say different things, many of the activist voices are actually saying the same things differently.

Calling for another 'new paradigm' based on 'the realization of a decentralized communal society . . . spontaneity and experimentation', Grabow and Heskin (1973, pp. 109—12) — evidently in an attack on, among other things, the weakness of large groups (which was cited by Harvey) — redefine planning as a '*synthesis* of rational action and spontaneity: evolutionary social experimentation within the context of an ecological ethic'.

Simmie (1974, p. 220) adds a more tempered and reflective voice which accurately represents the problems facing the activist planner:

In exposing the importance of the distributional consequences of town planning only the incidence of gains and losses may be measured technically. When it comes to deciding how they *ought to be distributed* between different groups, one enters the realms of social and political philosophy. When it comes to deciding *to distribute* differential gains and losses, then one is firmly in the realm of practical politics.

How activist planners cope with this problem of practical politics remains enigmatic. Some theorists, like (the now self-professed 'socialist') Harvey, argue for the expansion of consciousness posed by Marx and Engels (1974) in *The German Ideology*. Unlike the advocates' 'question of conscience', this effort is not aimed at an understanding of society itself. Its purpose is the construction of a 'revolutionary theory of urban activity' based on 'an analysis of the process of urbanization as a *producer* of contradictions within the total structure of the social formation, and as a specific *location* of contradiction within that social formation' (Massey, 1974, p. 235).[11] This longer term means of seeking a 'truly equitable' or 'socially just' social result which does not conflict with the immediate social result of the planner's work is currently much in dispute, particularly among the political 'left', which predominantly constitutes the activist view.[12] In terms of the manifestation of the activist view in the workplace, there have been some instances where planners have sought successfully to extend the economic and political franchise of less powerful social groups, usually by fighting *against* implementation of a plan which would result in some disbenefit accruing to those groups.[13]

One of the most recent and perhaps most controversial moves which have been taken under what appears to be an activist banner has been that of the planners in the Cleveland (Ohio) City Planning Commission. In its recent public report, the Commission's planners

> publicly present themselves not as disinterested arbiters of the public interest, but as committed actors who have chosen sides, and chosen sides with the least well-off in the city . . . They disavow a view of their role as having to do with long term decision-making, and instead present themselves as pragmatic activists, guided by political commitment and armed with technical skills to do battle on a range of policy issues in the name of the City's poor. (Piven, 1975, p. 309.)

This commitment is derived from an explicit understanding of town planning as a process for guiding the *resolution* of 'urban class conflict

. . . by actively preparing for protracted participation and vocal intervention in decision-making processes'.

The controversial nature of this stance does not derive from the
'commitment' to the 'least well-off', but from the view of town
planning as a medium for the resolution of class conflict. In my view,
this seems to bring us right back — full circle — to the neutralist purposes of Ackoff and the coalescing 'public interest' of the advocates.
Does not resolution of conflict presuppose common grounds upon
which the conflicting actors can agree? Does not 'protracted participation' in established decision-making processes assume a
pluralistic power structure? Is not the view of planning as a method
for resolving apparent social conflicts, particularly when emphasising
immediate benefits, closely in line with the legitimatory and stabilising
functions which Habermas attributes to town planning as a market
interventionist activity of the state?

Certainly, not all the views of town planning which I have
categorised as activist, nor all of the social theory which underlies
them, present the same dangerously circular front of the Cleveland
Planning Commission; not even most of them do. But the connection
between neutralist, advocate and activist views and purposes in town
planning remains. All three views and their associated planning roles
are built on a fundamental concern with the distribution component
of planning work, almost entirely to the exclusion of planning's
contribution to production.

Purpose in Planning: A Critique

There is a lot of grey in between the white and black of neutrality,
advocacy and activism. What I have tried to do in the review above
is to expose the range and, at the same time, the commonality of the
socio-political thinking which influences planning theory and work.

My own views of society and of how town planning functions
within society lead me to reject outright the neutralist and advocate
stances. I hold neither to a belief that one can separate political
influences from action nor to a concept of a common interest in
capitalist society. Further, while my own political arguments do
bear some similarity to those posed by the activitists, I also reject
the activist stance as a basis for a planning role. I believe that the
common distributive theme of the social theory which underlies
mainstream planning theory, to which the activist view adheres, is
inadequate as a basis for planning practice and planning action and
thus inappropriate for a planning role which reflects my own thinking.

Those groups which currently exercise controlling economic and political power in society can and do employ that power to claim increasingly larger shares of any benefits of planning. Simmie (1974, p. 143) has summarised this view well, writing that 'since the market has already produced an inegalitarian society by its hidden regressive mechanisms of redistribution, there is no reason to suppose that these mechanisms will not operate on the extra produce of economic growth [which planning facilitates]'. As a result, I do agree that the main *distributive* effect of public planning has been 'to keep the poor or a higher proportion of them poorer' (Hall, 1972, p. 267).

However, the composition and pattern of the urban public services toward which town planning is directed is 'established with the social means of production, with the character of the productive relations and social structure. The plans of cities will express . . . the class nature of society' (Ljobo, 1949, p. 95, quoted in Fisher, 1962). Dominant power holders in any society are those who control the material forces of production, and town planning thus reflects the existing composition of economic and political power and, in another sense, actually operates to maintain it. Accepting this relationship, I must reject the notion put forward by theorists like Seely (1962, p. 93) who implicitly take for granted existing production relationships and explicitly believe that planning 'presupposes that it [i.e., some future distribution of goods and services] is in some sense "open", that is, that actions, in some sense free, in "this now" affect "that then" '.

The Common Concern with Distribution

Town planning is a mechanism by which the owners of capital, through the administration of the state, can seek to improve conditions for continued production. Town planning can thus facilitate production. Planning work, then, clearly has two economic components. One component consists of a plan for an increase or recomposition of resources and the other component consists of a plan for the distribution of those resources. Planning work can be seen as a series of activities, some facilitating production, some facilitating distribution, and some facilitating both. The point to note, however, is that there is a profit or benefit which accrues from production *regardless of how the product is distributed*. Production dominates distribution.

Understanding the socio-political condition of planning work must be based on a consideration of who profits and of whose purpose is fulfilled by the social results of *both* components of planning work.

Yet, the difference between the neutralist, advocate and activist views of planning are formed by answers to questions which relate *only* to the distribution of benefits and resources. Few planning theories, irrespective of socio-political views which they reflect, offer critiques of the condition of planning work which include an analysis of the production component.

As Cockburn (1977) argued, non-owners of capital do benefit from the distribution to them of the improved social and material conditions which planning may effect. But given the political-economic basis of town planning within a capitalist society, even the activist role of adopting 'explicit, specific and accurate policies for progressive re-distribution in the spatial structure' (Simmie, 1974, p. 144) will have little effect on the resource-ownership which controls planning and society as a whole unless the forces which already dominate social power relationships are altered. Short of this difficult non-plannable task, existing power groups will determine the balance of wealth — and power — distribution in the short term. In the longer term, only social struggles — on a class basis — and consciousness-raising social forces — such as sexual and racial liberation movements — will affect the power structure; the ownership and the distribution of all produced benefits will necessarily change accordingly.

Planning, Planners and Production

Ownership and control over the means of production is the basis of economic and political power. Distribution of the benefits of planning according to the claims of existing power groups can be seen to result, therefore, in increased power for those with the most powerful claims. Simmie (1974, p. 143), again speaking of the distribution of the produce of economic growth, argues that 'if the top 10 per cent of the population own 50 per cent of personal wealth and the bottom 90 per cent own the other 50 per cent, this is not *a priori* reason for expecting that the fruits of growth will be distributed differently'. But although this distributional argument suggests that those groups holding controlling economic and political power would not settle for proportionately equal controlling shares of the benefits of public goods growth, it is clearly not always in their present interest to do so.

One of the capital-owning class's principal interests, certainly, is to maintain dominant power. Any explicit apportionment of increased economic growth which would further oppress the relative economic power base of other social groups could be counter-productive, particularly should it be seen to result in further arousing what Marx (1970a, p. 715) has called the 'rebellious indignation' of the oppressed class to a point where the 'expropriators are expropriated'. Consequently, moves to increase the market's regressive tendencies, while offering short-term gain to the capital-owning class, may be avoided in their long-term interest.

But this is not to say that dominant power groups do not otherwise gain increased shares of the benefits of planning in less explicit ways. The groups which make up what may be called the 'ruling class' are those which control the material forces of society. Marx and Engels (1974, p. 64) proposed, moreover, that

> the class which has the means of material production at its disposal, has control at the same time over the means of mental production, so that thereby, generally speaking, the ideas of those who lack the means of mental production are subject to it. The ruling ideas are nothing more than the ideal expression of the dominant material relationships, the dominant material relationships grasped as idea; hence of the relationships which make the one class the ruling one, therefore, the ideas of its dominance ... Insofar, therefore, as they rule as a class and determine the extent and compass of an epoch, it is self-evident that they do this in its whole range, hence among other things rule also as thinkers, as producers of ideas, and regulate the production and distribution of the ideas in their age: thus their ideas are the ruling ideas of the epoch.

This production of ruling ideas is legitimisation.

One of the ways in which ruling groups make claims on planning's benefits is by producing the ruling ideas of society. By defining 'synthesized social and economic needs' which planning work is meant to meet, dominant power groups can ensure their own direct benefit.[14] As a result, regardless of how the benefits of planning are distributed, it is to the profit of the capital-owning class to encourage town planning because planning helps to maintain existing production relationships. By improving conditions required for continued production, planning benefits those who dominate production relationships – that is, the owners of capital – either directly by the *type* of benefit produced (for example, decreased reproduction costs of labour in housing) or indirectly by ensuring their power positions remain safe because of the satiated 'needs' of other groups (through the provision, for example, of recreational facilities).

Now, there is another factor which comes into play in considering the relationship between production and town planning. That is the collective influence of the self interests of individual planners. The relative power of the planning profession over its own activities is minor in the light of the control exercised by the state employer. By not questioning the real aims of the state's planning activity — that is, by not questioning its relationship to production — planners are able to enjoy some range of control over their distribution-oriented activities where it really does not conflict with the purposes of capital as formalised through the state administration. Planners end up toying only with the formalised and propagandised aims of the state activity. Within this range of 'false-control', the self-interest of individual planners plays an important role, right into the hands of the legitimatory agents of social power holders.

This self-interest is directed toward strengthening the planner's position as controller of the functional development of publicly-employed services — that is, toward strengthening the position of *a* planner as *the* planner. By assuming, unquestioningly, the responsibility for planning 'needed' commodities and services, town planners may attempt to strengthen their own planning control or to extend their own authorised responsibility beyond the scope or timing of any immediate planning brief. This exercise may be directed toward ensuring a continuation or an increase in the actual capacity to plan which planners currently enjoy. This may be done either by making further planning contingent upon the planners' own partici-pation or by suppressing threats of increased planning capabilities or authorities by other groups apparently competing for planning control.

The planner's personal self-interest, which is largely influenced by the nature of capitalist social ideology, derives from a presumption on the part of the planners, as demonstrated in mainstream planning theory, that the traditional town planning process can lead to an end bigger than planning itself; that, as a result of a con-tinuum of planning work, some public welfare or social justice will be attained. The activists' conception of themselves as some sort of agents of social change epitomises this point. The 'means' to whatever 'bigger end' is sought consists of the role which the planner assumes in distributing 'needed' commodities and services. *But without a commodity or service to (plan to) distribute there is no means and there is no end.* (Recall Handler's 'Planning of any kind is possible only when a surplus exists'.)

So, by not questioning the production component of planning work, town planners allow themselves the manifestation of neutralist, advocate and activist stances. But they also implicitly condone the mechanisms which sustain the very power base which makes such manifestations structurally insignificant. By working as if the individual planner and as if planning — in and of themselves — can 'make a difference' town planners further support the legitimatory actions of the state and lend strength to what Lukes termed the third dimension of power — the ability to submerge conflict and mask real interests — which the dominant capital-owning class enjoys.

The Planner's Role

The town planner, as an individual, is not the agent of social change, is not the champion of the common interest.

> The final causes of all social changes and political revolutions are to be sought not in man's brains, not in man's better insight into external truth and justice, but in changes in the modes of production and exchange. (Engels, 1974, pp. 57–8.)

That is, in changes in the structural basis of society, a basis which changes only with protracted struggle.

The role of the town planner must be one which recognises this ineffectiveness at an individual level. It must be one which seeks, rather, 'to impart . . . a full knowledge of the conditions and of the meaning of the momentous act' of social change (Engels, 1974, p. 79), to oneself, to other planners and to social groups whose own 'momentous action' is assuaged often by town planning itself.

But the planner, like all workers, must work, in a workplace in which such collectivist-oriented consciousness-raising can only be done surreptitiously, if not subversively. So what can the planner do to directly manifest this socio-political purpose — that is, seeking historical change in the ownership of the means of production — in planning action?

Rosenhead (1976b, p. 271) suggests questions which may guide the actions of operational research workers toward this purpose:

> First, whether the practical effect is to increase the exploitation or control of the workers employed by the client; and second, whether the ideological effect is to increase mystification as to the

structural relationships which dominate social life, or to increase the
sense of powerlessness of the people *vis-à-vis* the vested interests . . .
If the answer to any of these questions is 'yes', then the work must
be regarded with suspicion.

These same questions can be applied directly to the work of town
planners. The actions which the individual planner takes, should the
answers be 'yes', can only depend upon the immediate situation. But
if the social result of planning work aids dominant capitalist power-
holders in the 'control or co-optation of conflict' a choice must be
made 'as to which side [of social conflict] we are on' (p. 271).

In my view, this area of conflict control is where the planner's role
is most important. One of the most insidious aspects of town planning
as an exercise of the political power of the capital-owning class is the
submergence of conflict, often through false-conflict resolution. Town
planning is an instrument, of the capital-owning class, for conflict
control or co-optation or favourable resolution, because town planning,
in the late capitalist social structure,

> is *defined* as a means of directing change 'toward the ultimate
> objective of orderly and harmonious community processes' or as
> 'methods and techniques to coordinate and bring into harmony' the
> uses of land and the structures on it. [But] . . . harmony, one
> must note, equals stagnation, or lack of progress. Change takes
> place because a disjunction arises among the parts of an inter-
> related system and a planner who wants to bring about more or
> different changes cannot dispense with this motive power.
> (Peterson, 1966, p. 141.)

I disagree with Peterson on a number of points, but he is correct in
saying that the 'motive power' of change in town planning is disjunction,
simply put, conflict. If the planner's purpose is to facilitate social
change in the way in which society is organised and, therefore, in the
distribution of power, he or she should not rush to *resolve* conflict
but rather to *expose* it, if not promote it, as a force for change.
Planning work is not a 'means to an end' but an end in itself — the
end of politicising planning work, the end of exposing and promoting
social conflict as a mechanism, in its own right, for change in the social
power structure.

Although conflict can be employed in planning through decisions
which relate to the development of public service systems, the planner

must not suffer the illusion that decisions which expose or promote conflict in 'public service planning' will in themselves cause or result in significant social change. Planning work may well force the exposure of local conflicts over 'the spatial structure'; planning work may even contribute to a material gain and to a political consciousness-raising for working class groups which benefit from struggles to obtain state-financed local services. But planning work will not result in direct change in the social power structure. Planning work simply can *not* achieve that, no matter how long the work's continuum. Only the social power holders' own forced participation and struggle within conflict situations will alter the distribution of power. Planning work can only be an aid to that historical process. It certainly can not replace it as an agent of social change.

Notes

1.　It may be argued that the less mechanistic or predetermined is an individual's work, the more opportunity the worker has to manifest in different ways his or her attitude as an individual within the workplace. A machine operator, for example, whose view of the social result of work leads to a personal rejection of the perceived aims of the work-institution has few roles through which he or she can individually manifest this within the workplace – evasion, resignation and revolt being the most apparent (see Andrieux and Lignon, 1960, quoted in Bottomore, 1965). A teacher with the same attitude, on the other hand, enjoys other opportunities to manifest rejection – for example, assuming the role of 'classroom subversive' (see Postman and Weingartner, 1971) – without risking the dismissal in which a less subtle disruption on the machine floor would most likely result.

The availability of these options to the worker corresponds with the status and with the security within the workplace which workers such as machine operators and teachers have. These derive, in turn, from the structural power enjoyed by particular occupational groups.

Other variables broaden the range of roles which the individual can assume: collective action, the opportunity to voice attitude in and out of the workplace, and the views and actions (particularly legitimatory actions) of those who directly formulate the formal aims of the work-institution are among them.

2.　Harvey (1973) suggests that the time of value for such studies is passed. Speaking of empirical investigations of the social conditions in urban ghettos he says, 'mapping even more evidence of man's patent inhumanity to man is counter-revolutionary in the sense that it allows the bleeding-heart liberal in us to pretend we are contributing to a solution when in fact we are not . . . it merely serves to expiate guilt without our ever being forced to face the fundamental issues, let alone do anything about them' (pp. 144–5).

3.　Attempts to agree on a definition of planning theory present problems of their own. Perhaps the most popular, but least illuminating, definition is Faludi's (1973) which distinguishes between theories *of* planning and theories *in* planning. In a comprehensive survey article, Friedmann and Hudson (1974) identify four major traditions of planning theory: (1) philosophical synthesis, aimed at achieving integrated multi-disciplinary views of planning as a social process; (2) the tradition of rationalism, concerned with how decisions can be made more rationally; (3) the tradition of organisation development, focused on ways to achieve changes in organisational structure and behaviour; and (4) the tradition of empiricism, emphasising the measurement of system behaviour as it actually exists.

4.   Beckman (1964, p. 326) saw the role of the planner in very much the same light as Walker:

> He [the planner] is a team player. His loyalty to the politician must be that of a disciplined soldier in combat who has been trained to know that while his commanding officer will protect him to the extent possible, he is nevertheless expendable, both as an individual and as part of a unit . . . He must develop his instinct for self-preservation to the highest possible point. He cannot afford to make mistakes. The consequence to himself, his agency, and the elected official may be too serious.

5.   Ackoff's early arguments (1974b) along this line are addressed specifically to operational researchers and 'management scientists'. As Ackoff (1976) has expanded his argument, more recently to include an attempt to synthesise Plato and Aristotle, he has begun speaking to the wider audience of all 'professionals' who design or plan 'social systems'.

6.   Ackoff, in turn, denies 'structural conflict as the dominant feature of social organization' (Rosenhead, 1976b, p. 270). Ackoff and Rosenhead have argued at length over the former's work. Rosenhead, who sees social conflict as presenting a potential for social change, argues that planners or management scientists whose work within some organisational 'system' is directed toward producing common goals 'do *not* . . . have a primary role to play as agents of social change' (p. 271).

7.   Handler's argument is an important one because it calls into question, as those of few other planning theorists have done, the production aspects of planning work. Although I disagree with Handler's capitalist formulations, I think it is unfortunate that little attention was paid to his case for the development of planning theory on the basis of economic analysis. Such a development may have broken planning theory out of its self-imposed isolation from other socio-political analyses.

8.   Views of the social results of planning work and their respective manifestations in the workplace cannot be isolated from debates over planning *methods* which simultaneously occupy much of the forum of planning theory (see 3.) and which also seek to make planning more rational. While people such as Altshuler (1965) and Friedmann (1965) argued whether or not unquestioning acceptance of the political controls of the city is a prerequisite for planning success, others such as Meyerson (1956) and Etzioni (1967) argued the alternative merits of comprehensive planning methods, incremental planning methods and methods inbetween. This continuing methodological debate should not be regarded as value-free, despite arguments about depoliticising planning methods in order to distinguish 'between professional *objectivity* (meaning processes for getting things right and introducing checks, validation procedures and so on) and professional commitment' (Cowan, 1973, p. 5). Webber's (1968–9, p. 295) 'permissive planning' method, for example, is based on the conception that 'planning is inside the political system, and, hence a growing political force in itself'. Ackoff's idealised future planning is based on a seemingly neutral, or at least non-discriminatory, 'love for all'.

One of the more significant influences in the attempts to depoliticise planning methods has come from the application of recent approaches in organisation behaviour. Beginning with the work of Lippitt, Watson and Westley (1958), organisation development treated planning

> not as an intellectual process of efficiently adopting means to given ends, but as primarily a method for including change . . . The operating principle of organization and development is that any lasting change in process and structure must come from within the organization and involve far-reaching changes in awareness, attitude, behaviour, and values on the part of its constituents . . . Planners may be instrumental as catalysts in the process, guiding the ongoing learning in accord with its inner dynamics. (Friedmann and Hudson, 1974, p. 10.)

Although organisational development clearly regards the planner as a sort of change agent, change is not seen as a socio-political phenomenon but rather as an inherent characteristic of organisational development. The planner is seen as an expert who 'uses his own person and the relationships that he jointly builds, adapts and terminates with the client system . . . as major tools in liberating, informing, and empowering the client to deal more aptly with itself (or himself) and its (or his) worlds' (Bennis *et al.*, 1969, p. 371). Some planning theorists, like Friedman, and methodologists, like Friend, Power and Yewlett (1974), have built on the inter-active aspects of these arguments to develop methods which make planning bureaucracies work in ways which they view as more efficient, more objective and more rational. (I am indebted to Jonathan Rosenhead for leading me to consider the political nature of the inter-activist approach to planning.)

9. The requirement of an *expansion* of the professional responsibilities of planners in order to assume a political role derives from the continued assumption, on the part of planning theorists, that *town planning* is somehow divorced from the political and social conditions which are manifest in the state organisation. This is not to say that town planners — specifically, advocates and activists — do not see planning as political activity when *they* do it; but there seems to be an implicit assumption in the literature that before advocates and activists came along town planning was not *really* political.

10. Because power affects all distribution within the commodity and labour market, the powerful could further strengthen their own position through an ability to claim — via wage bidding — the services of highly skilled 'non-aligned' or neutralist planners (see Simmie, 1974, p. 155).

11. Massey criticises Harvey's self-claimed 'liberal' to 'socialist' transformation (*Social Justice and the City*), arguing that while Harvey has opened up 'the debate of a new structure for the study of urbanization' he leaves the overall impression that 'the break from the initial problematic of liberalism and humanism has not been entirely achieved'. (1974, p. 235.)

12. Some theorists, echoing the sentiments of the utopian socialists, argue that 'planning was foreign to Marx's thought' (Peterson, 1966, p. 132) in the light of the inevitable consequences of historical realism. Others attempt to go 'beyond Marx'. Grabow and Heskin (1973, p. 112) argue, 'Change must take place in all realms . . . It is no longer productive to claim the right way to make a revolution'. I think Lenin might have agreed until Grabow and Heskin go on to say:

> The answer will not be found in either the seizure of power nor in the destruction of all power . . . The revolution is where you are, and it is what we are becoming: consciousness and action merge. Martin Buber was perhaps

more eloquent: 'Just as I do not believe in Marx's "gestation" of the new form, so I do not believe in Bakunin's virgin birth from the womb of revolution. But I do believe in the meeting of idea and fate in the creative hour.' (1973, p. 138).

13. It may be argued that where planners have managed 'successes' for less powerful groups, they have been allowed by controlling power groups. The planner's political activity often takes the form of securing increased participation of less powerful groups in negotiating shares of the benefits of planning. However, by including the voices of these less powerful groups in negotiations of 'relatively slight consequence', more powerful groups can covertly expropriate what power the former groups do have as a sanction of their own decision-making and controlling roles. These token conflicts also serve as a way through which power holders can deflect weaker interest-groups' potential power from more threatening activity.

It is interesting to note, however, that fighting *against* a plan's implement-ation – exemplified in the battles over Covent Garden and St Agnes Place (Lambeth) – calls into question not only the distribution of benefits of a plan but also the production of benefits altogether.

14. At worst – for the 'ruling class' – these ruling ideas will result in what Glazer (1965, p. 24) has called 'controlled revolution' wherein the capital-owning class allows interests of other groups to be met, again, in an effort to protect the former's own longer term interest.

Part Two

PLANNING AND HEALTH SERVICES

3 HEALTH SERVICES PLANNING – THE LIMITS OF ACTION SPACE

This chapter and the next one are concerned with particular forms of planning action in health services provision. I will temporarily set aside considerations of the planner's role in order to discuss, in general and through example, the other dimensions of planning action – that is, what the planner plans (action space) and what the planner does to plan (operational activities).

A considerable amount of literature already exists – exemplified in the writings of Navarro (1976), Hart (1971b), Renaud (1975), Kelman (1975), and Krause (1977), among others – which offer variably incisive understandings of the political-economy of health and of health services in capitalist societies. It is not my intent to replicate those efforts here. Instead, I will try to provide an overview of the health services planners' workplace, of the range of issues which planners face, of the tasks which planners undertake, and of the arguments – sometimes political and often only regarded as peripheral – which complicate health services planners' work.

There is a great deal of confusion about the work of health services planners. Indeed, some question whether health services planning exists as a truly definable 'effective' and 'rational' process at all. Krause (1977, p. 239), for example, points out that 'the field is essentially undeveloped and undifferentiated, and the process is very much an *ad hoc* activity'. Part of the questioning and confusion may derive from a tendency to confuse terms like 'health planning' or 'medical planning' with 'health services planning', and *vice versa*. The distinction is not merely semantic, and to avoid confusion here a definition of health services planning is required. But any study of health services planning, however defined, must be set, first, against a more important distinction between health and medicine, a distinction which is now customarily made in health literature and in lay discussion alike.

Health and Medicine

When we talk about health in society today, we consider its death-rate or the life-span of its members. When we talk about the provision of health we talk about it as a social service – something which can be added to a community if there are sufficient facilities, hospitals, drugs, scalpels and men to wield them. At one moment we think of ourselves as healthy, able to work, to meet our commitments and carry out our responsibilities, to escape work and enjoy our leisure; at the next moment we are sick. Like a dirty pound note, we are taken out of circulation. We are sent to bed or to hospital, for between health and disease there is nothing. (Rossdale, 1965, p. 82.)

In the years since this then-radical observation, a great deal has been expounded, purportedly to fill the gap between understanding health and understanding disease. The machine and causal models of man and disease, which Rossdale blamed in part for the 'dirty pound note' social attitude toward 'the sick', have been publicly challenged as the basis for understanding health, even by the professional and institutional groups which Rossdale saw as promoting them in the first place.

An *ecological* conception of health has emerged, in which health is seen as 'the product of a harmonized relationship between man and his ecology' (Rossdale, p. 87). This ecological view has become the platform, and seemingly the common understanding, upon which much of the prevailing discussion about health is made. It serves as the topic for World Health Organisation publications (WHO, 1975), for portfolio economic analyses (Dowie, 1975), and for popular public reading.

Many observers (e.g. Dubos, 1959; Powles, 1973; McKeown and Lowe, 1966; Hetzel, 1974; and others) have pointed out the historical influences upon health of environmental changes in advanced industrial societies. In fact, measured against the effects of social reforms in such areas as housing, pollution and sanitation during the last 150 years, the impact of medicine upon health has been small.

In the United States, for example, the middle nineteenth century mortality rate from tuberculosis, a leading cause of death, was estimated to be approximately 500 per 100,000 persons per year.

By 1900 the death rate in the US had fallen to slightly less than 200 deaths per 100,000 people per year. Thereafter there was a strong, steady decline to a rate of 2.8 in 1969 . . . [Even though] no immunization against tuberculosis has been adopted in the US (Dingle, 1973, p. 55).[1]

Similar historical patterns have occurred, in Europe and North America, for scarlet fever, measles, whooping cough and typhoid fever.

> The decline of those infections in which specific [medical] measures are widely believe [sic] to have been effective — smallpox, syphilis, tetanus and possibly diphtheria — made only a small contribution to the total fall of the death rate ... It was not until the twentieth century and probably not until 1935, with the introduction of sulphonamides that specific medical measures became available which were sufficiently powerful to reduce mortality from infection to an extent that would have influenced the national [in this case, British] death rate. (McKeown, 1976, p. 4.)

During the latter part of this century, however, the emphasis has shifted away from looking at changing environmental and behavioural factors as *contributors* to 'good health' towards recognising them as potential *detractors* from 'good health'.[2] The spread of urbanisation, for example, which brought with it public sanitation and a direct reduction in typhus and other filth-borne fevers in the nineteenth century, is now seen as a major contributor to respiratory disease and mental depression, among other ailments (see WHO, 1972). Behavioural practices previously were studied and credited with responsibility for *improvements in health*; change in reproductive practice, which restricted population growth, is an example. Now other behavioural practices are more carefully studied as leading *contributors to death*; cigarette smoking and automobile accidents are cited as two of the major factors. Indeed, an ever-increasing amount of concern given health's 'harmonised relationship' centres on individual responsibilities for personal health as well as for human ecology.

Employing the index of mortality as an admittedly inadequate measure of health, Hart (1971b, pp. 327—8) has identified a range of 'separate though interdependent variables' upon which changes in health depend:

> First, social and environmental changes: housing, wages, nutrition, education, working conditions, and the customary forms of social behaviour that make up culture ...
> The second factor is the level attained by medical science ...
> The third factor is the extent to which scientific possibility is translated into social fact — the delivery of medical care.

The list of biological and social factors which are recognised as inter-dependently affecting human health now encompasses virtually all aspects of what has become called 'the human environment'. Amongst these, as Venediktov's (1976) illustrative summary shows, 'medical science' is one small sector of a total social and biological environment in which other factors, such as 'climate', 'nutrition' and 'industry', share at least equal importance in regard to personal health. The label 'health field' (Lalonde, 1974) has come to connote not merely medicine, but a wide range of social, behavioural and biological conditions which influence health. If it were to be based solely on the ecological conception of health, medicine's role in health would appear to be waning.

However, despite the liberal redefinition of health, there remains an important distinction between the ecological conception of health as a definition and the conception of health in practical applications. Medicine, as a curative and therapeutic activity, remains the dominant focus in the health field, not only for capitalist society's control of health services organisation and expenditure,[3] but also for the in-dividual's conception of health. For the person requiring health services, the dominance can be at least partially explained by the immediate life-threat posed by the physical and mental diseases and injuries which medicine is supposed to treat. This in turn has resulted in what Cochrane (1972, p. 8) identifies as 'the layman's uncritical belief in the ability of the medical profession at least to help if not to cure'. He continues:

> The basis for this was probably the doctor's ability to reduce pain, the general placebo effect, the tendency of many diseases to dis-appear spontaneously, or improve with time, and the higher education and social status which possibly assisted him in alleviating hysterical symptoms . . . This led slowly to the very widespread belief that for every symptom or group of symptoms there was a bottle of medicine, a pill, an operation, or some other therapy which would at least help.

'People expect their doctors to keep them healthier — and even happier' (*The Economist*, 25 Oct. 1975, p. 11). Often contributing to this expectation is media sensationalism associated with advances in medical science. International headlines of Salk's poliomyelitis vaccine, of Barnard's heart transplants and, more recently, of Steptoe's 'test tube' baby are examples; 'space medicine' and other technological developments, particularly those in diagnostic and surgical services, have attracted similar attention. The visibility and political appeal of buildings and equipment which accommodate and facilitate medical services — as compared to often less politically attractive actions such as pollution control or automobile safety regulations — support the dominant image of medicine as health, despite concerns for a harmonised human ecology.

Partially as a result of this, medicine and providers of medical care, although historically minor contributors to what may be regarded as 'good health', have continued to enjoy a powerful position in defining health in practice. Recently, however, more direct attacks on medicine's position in health have emerged from ecological health advocates and these attacks have become the centre of a growing health provider-health consumer debate.

Challenging Medicine's Control over 'Health'

Certainly not the only, but perhaps the most popular, critique of 'medicine as health' has come from Ivan Illich (1975). Illich argues in his book, *Medical Nemesis*, that 'the medical establishment has become a major threat to health' (p. 11), not only because of the iatrogenic illnesses which result from often ineffective, overeffective or inefficient medicine, but also because of the 'medicalization of life'. In Illich's view, the 'medicalization of life' has resulted from the industrialisation of western societies. To overcome what he terms the resultant 'social' and 'structural' iatrogeneses, Illich's two-fold suggestion is for society to set limits on industrial growth and for individuals to simultaneously assume responsibility for their own self-care:

> since medicine is a sacred cow, its slaughter would have a 'vibration effect': people who can face suffering and death with-out need for magicians and mystagogues are free to rebel against other forms of expropriation now practised by teachers, engineers, lawyers, priests and party officials. (p. 161.)[4]

Hostility towards the 'mystical' control which medicine and the medical profession have historically exercised over the definition of health is now widespread. Many of Illich's arguments, in fact, repeat those which have been voiced several times in the past decade. Friedson (1970, p. 251), for example, in his study of the medical profession and its exercise of social control, stated that 'the medical profession has first claim to jurisdiction over the label of illness and anything to which it may be attached, irrespective of its capacity to deal with it effectively'. Zola (1971, p. 175) later categorised this 'attaching process' in four ways:

> first, through the expansion of what in life is deemed relevant to the good practice of medicine; secondly, through the retention of absolute control over certain technical procedures; thirdly, through the retention of near absolute access to certain 'taboo' areas; and finally, through the expansion of what in medicine is deemed relevant to the good practice of life.

In 1975, the Director-General of the World Health Organisation brought the attack on the medical profession home to roost:

> The wave of social consciousness in the 19th century in Europe and in North America broadened our understanding of 'Health' but resulted in a reaction by the medical Establishment and a construction which is still continuing. By legislation, by training, by organisation, and by the way in which health-related interventions are stated and restricted, there has been a progressive 'mystification' in medical care which is continuing almost unchecked. As our understanding of cause and effect has grown, 'medicine' has continued to restrict the range of problems for which it considers itself responsible and the gap between 'health care' and 'medical care' has become ever wider. This has been coupled with an organisational change which has influenced the manner of dealing with these problems, a gross restriction in the information available and decisions to be made by people outside the health professions, and an unnecessary but inevitable dependency of the population upon the holders of these mysteries. (Mahler, 1975, p. 829.)

The self-control of physicians' work — what Johnson (1972) termed professional 'collegiate control'[5] — results from an ability of physicians to define the needs of consumers. As Abel-Smith (1976, p. 46) has pointed out, 'the main demand for the use of health resources comes mainly from the doctor'. He goes on to remark that the 'dominating feature of the health market is the consumers' lack of knowledge. They do not know the risks of ill-health. They do not normally know what precise services they want to buy' (p. 56). The doctor does; and the consumer-patient, who infrequently requires medical services and who is often too ill at the times of requiring such services to question their precision, as a result 'trusts the doctor with the key to the medicine cabinet' (Illich, 1975, p. 32).

> Very few industries could be named where the consumer is so dependent upon the producer for information concerning the quality of the product. In the typical case he is even subject to the producer's recommendation concerning the quantity to be purchased. A recent report by the American Medical Association says flatly, 'The "quantity" of hospital services consumed in 1962 was determined by physicians'. (Fuchs, 1967, pp. 329–30.)

So, despite arguments challenging the control of the medical profession over health, when individuals require medical care and when medical care is provided, the very nature of the professional-client relationship mutes the challenge in practice.[6]

Within the context of all of these definitions and debates, health care delivery is the provision to individual clients of medical and other health services at a specific point of consumption. The work of health services planners is to prescribe the physical and spatial means for providing these services. As such, within the bounds of the health-medicine distinction, within the ecological health field, the action space of health services planning more closely associates with medical care.

What Health Services Planners Plan

In defining the action space of planners' work, Underwood (1976) distinguished between *occupied* action space, on the one hand, and *potential, diffuse* and *debated* action spaces on the other hand. Occupied action space is 'the range of issues and situations over which they [i.e. planners] are recognized regularly to exercise authority' (p. 6). Potential, diffuse and debated action spaces connote the ranges of issues and situations which planners aspire to affect, indirectly or unintentionally affect, and unauthoritatively affect, respectively. What the latter three ranges of issues have in common, and what distinguishes them from the range of issues comprised in occupied action space, is the lack of authority which is invested in planners to concern themselves with these issues in practice.[7]

In relation to health services planning, a confusion between occupied action space and, what may be termed, for the sake of simplicity, 'unoccupied action space', in theory, reflects itself in a misunderstanding of what health services planners can, and do, do in reality. This results partly from a preponderance of argument, in academic programmes and in the literature, which urge the concentration in one workplace of decision-making related to everything from the definition of health to the financial organisation of medical services to the location of community health centres. Sometimes this wide range of activity is titled 'health planning'; other times, 'health services planning'. But the simple point is this: nowhere in capitalist societies (or in any other industrialised social organisation, for that matter) is planning conducted on all fronts of the health field in such a concentrated manner, irrespective of the political and economic administration of health services. Health services planning work in Britain is similar to, if not the same as, health services planning work in the United States or Australia or France. Planning the physical and spatial delivery of health services is an almost generic activity, an activity which is conducted at a low level — both politically and demographically — in the state's administrative hierarchy of policy- and decision-making. This is not to say the delineation of action space always and everywhere results in a precise 'occupied'/ 'unoccupied' distinction. It *is* to say, however, the planners who plan the provision of health services do *not* regularly plan financial organisation or administrative structure of the health system. More importantly, they do not plan health.

The Provision of Health Services

In the United States, where total spending on medical care in 1975 accounted for 8.4 per cent of GNP (Russell and Burke, 1978) and where public spending alone rose by 15.6 per cent in 1976 (McKinlay, 1977), there have been, in response, many proposals for a planned financial reorganisation of medical and other health services. Observers who not too long ago were calling for nationalisation of medical insurance (e.g., Kennedy, 1972 and Ribicoff, 1972) are now leading advocates of health insurance legislation. Alternatively, there are arguments for improvements in private medical insurance (e.g., Feldstein, 1973) and for continued growth of privately financed health maintenance organisations and prepaid hospital and primary care services (Anderson and Robins, 1976), while a small and largely ignored number propose nationalisation of health services altogether (United States, 1978). There are even proposals to meet health care inadequacies through state financing of community healers, much along the lines of 'barefoot doctors' in China (Falk and Hawkins, 1975).

In Canada, where with public health insurance *per capita* health care expenditures are currently escalating at an annual rate of nearly 15 per cent (Bennett and Krasney, 1977), and in Australia, where nationalised health insurance was initiated in 1975 and then effectively dismantled the following year with a change in government, many of the same arguments abound.

In Britain the attention of health services observers has not focused so much on financial organisation, although there are cries for a return to private medicine (Jewkes, 1961; Powell, 1976). Rather, calls for improvements in the provision of medical and personal health services concentrate on allocation of financial resources to particular areas of care within the National Health Service (Castle, 1976; Owen, 1976), on administration of the service (Forsyth, 1973) and, more broadly, on quality of care (Cochrane, 1972).

Often, the proposals which emerge from these varied organisational and resource allocation studies are put forward as 'health planning' recommendations. Often, recommendations are detailed to include specifications of health manpower teams, of community-based services and even of building types. This is where the confusion arises concerning what health services planning does and does not address. This confusion is further complicated by the arguments surrounding the distinction between health and medicine; and by the collection of ambiguously-titled books which deal with the planned physical and spatial provision of medical services: *Health Planning* (Reinke, 1972), *Health Services Planning* (Dunnell, 1976) and *Planning for Health* (Blum, 1974) are three examples.

More than just a semantic confusion, this loose interchange of terminology tends to make the action space of health services planning work appear to encompass more than it actually does. Health services planners do not plan the legislative structure of health services provision, nor do they plan financial or administrative organisation, nor the quality of health care. Decisions regarding these types of issues, whether or not they are taken in no more than an *ad hoc* fashion, *are* taken at a formal political level within the state's administrative structure, reflecting directly the economic and social organisation within which the health services operate. Legislative, financial and administrative limits to health services provision are imposed upon health services planners, either as constraints or as directives which require implementation. Currently, for example, governmental directives to health services planning agencies emphasise economic efficiency, substitution of less expensive services for high cost services, and rationalisation of existing services.

Health services planners, then, plan the provision of health services at the point of consumption, within whatever organisational, financial and administrative frameworks exist as a result of the political-economic mechanisms of society. To undertake this task, health services planners specify the allocation of defined and limited ranges of resources to operationalise, facilitate and accommodate the production and supply of medical and other personal health services.

Now, health services can be regarded as physical and operational groupings of separate medical and non-medical tasks to meet specific health problems. These problems — putting aside definitions of 'illness' for now — are not always biological in nature, nor only disease-related. Some health problems, for example, are met by merely 'talking things over' between patient and physician — a service which, as Varlaam *et al.* (1972) have shown, forms an integral part of health care (cited in OHE, 1974). Health services are not provided only as therapeutic requirements. Health services are required and consumed in order to prevent health problems, to identify health problems when they occur, to intervene in the natural course of health problems towards recovery, and to alleviate the disabling effects of health problems. As physical tasks, health services require a wide range of resources, both capital and labour.

Fuchs (1967, pp. 332–3) has identified three broad components which render health services needed for personal consumption: labour ('personnel engaged in medical occupations'), physical capital ('plant and equipment used by this personnel') and intermediate goods and services ('i.e., drugs, bandages, purchased laundry services'). These are the resources which the health services planner allocates. But health services planning is 'not just concerned with the provision of buildings, facilities and staff. It needs to be used in the design and implementation of policies' (Dunnell and Holland, 1973, p. 233). So, the work of the health services planner is a means by which policies, which are established through the political and economic activities of society, and which sometimes are formalised within the institutional hierarchy of the health system, are carried into effect at the point of delivery.

The Operational Activities of Health Services Planning

Like the operational activities of the town planning process, the operational activities of health services planning have changed over time. Some of the change in health services planning activities is due to the employment of techniques developed largely in other forms of planning, a phenomenon attributed by some to a relative lack of sophistication of health services planning as a planning discipline (see Frieden and Peters, 1970, and Krause, 1977). But a great deal of the change in health services planning is owed to the historical shift in the focus of health services provision itself.

The Influence of Hospital Provision

Until the second quarter of this century, health services planning centred around considerations of the supply of hospitals in specific locations. The development of hospitals under the auspices of often charitable institutions had resulted in decades, if not centuries, of independently organised centres for serving 'the sick'.

Britain offers a fine example. Hospital provision found its roots in the late eighteenth century when voluntary hospitals and workhouses accommodated those persons who were ill and either without family or without finances to enable their being cared for at home. Although some of the voluntary hospitals remained from original construction in the twelfth and thirteenth centuries, the number of hospital facilities was to expand rapidly through the nineteenth century – nearly tripling between 1861 and 1891 alone. (Abel-Smith, 1964.)

This growth in hospital provision resulted primarily from three phenomena: (1) 'improvements in both medicine and nursing were making it more advantageous for the sick to be admitted'; (2) 'the campaign against outdoor relief' which consequently encouraged the poor sick to seek admission to hospital where they could receive free treatment and accommodation; and (3) 'the desire to isolate cases of infectious disease for the protection of the public at large' (pp. 152–3). Simultaneously contributing to the growth in hospitals was the rapid increase in population, particularly in urban areas, and the emergence of the strong professional interests in medical schools, which were associated with voluntary hospitals as sources of teaching and research material. But the lack of co-ordination between the various voluntary hospitals and local authorities, which had assumed responsibility for mental asylums, resulted in 'a pattern of hospitals which was unplanned, ill-coordinated, and based not so much upon the needs of the sick as upon the requirements of politics, economics, and professional interests' (Cowan, 1969, p. 36).

In 1900, 'hospitals were still regarded with dread by the vast majority of the population' (Abel-Smith, 1964, p. 152), even with the increase in specialised institutions and public authority control. The First World War accentuated the need for hospital based services in

Britain, however, and shortly afterwards the independent provision of
voluntary hospitals once again grew rapidly, this time aided by the
availability of private voluntary insurance. Despite this growth, however, it was not until the late 1930s that the Sankey Commission
proposed the imposition of a centralised co-ordinating structure over
public and voluntary hospital provision. This was the first attempt
in Britain at planning the supply of health services with a concern for
more than one facility at a time.[8] After the passage of the National
Health Service Act in 1946, approximately 3,600 hospitals in
Britain were taken into national ownership. (Godber, 1975.) A
study made in 1956 shoed that 45 per cent of the hospitals then in
the National Health Service had been originally constructed before
1891. (Abel-Smith and Titmuss, 1956.)

Many industrialised countries experienced the historical evolution
of similar unplanned patterns of medical services dominated by
hospital facilities (see Fry, 1969; Risley, 1962; Sax, 1972; Abel-
Smith, 1976; and Knowles, 1973). However, following the momentum
of the social welfare programmes introduced in attempts to offset
the economic crises of the 1930s, and with the conclusion of the
Second World War, many capitalist societies established planning as
a formal activity in health services systems.

The scope of health services planning concerns varied greatly
between countries. In England, for example, the imposition of a
nationally planned pattern of medical services under the National
Health Service affected hospital services and health services rendered
by general practitioners and local authorities as well. In the United
States, on the other hand, planning councils instituted under the
Hill-Burton Act of 1946 were authorised only to assess needs for new
hospital construction. (Stebbins and Williams, 1972.) In some countries,
such as Belgium and the Netherlands, planning concentrated on the
control of hospital provision through subsidy schemes; in others, such
as France and Denmark, plans for hospitals were implemented through
direct public provision. (Maynard, 1975.)

But whatever the range of authority, at the time that formalised
planning was introduced to health services provision most countries
were faced 'with an inheritance of plant which had evolved before
hospitals were rationally planned and cannot be discarded quickly'.
(Abel-Smith, 1976, p. 162.)[9] These 'inheritances' represented a considerable portion of national health care expenditure and capital, and,
as a result, a proportionately large amount of planning work was
directed towards making existing units more effective and efficient

within the policy framework of newly reorganised health systems. Of course, hospitals were not the only elements for consideration within health services plans. But the dominance of that particular building type — bringing with it high capital and operating costs — influenced health services planning to concentrate on hospital provision, often as the basis upon which other community-based health services were considered.

As a result, in the 1950s and early 1960s, plans for the provision of health services often began with the designation of specific building types in specific locations. These could be hospitals, hostels or health centres, on anything from community to national levels. Such plans — the 1964 Hospital Plan for England and Wales (Great Britain, 1964) is an example — were accompanied by a detailed consideration of what services those buildings were to accommodate. Buildings are easy to envisage, imply readily identifiable roles in a health care system and, consequently, are quite easily managed by both planning and funding decision-makers.

While private provision of hospitals continued on the basis of 'market assessments' and return to investment, plans for new public facilities were often based on apparent inadequacies of available health services, resulting from population growth or redistribution. Ratios of acute beds provided per thousand population, for example, served with population forecasts as guides by which inter-regional comparisons could be made and requirements for new hospital beds could be established. The result was that much of the effort of health services planning was spent on 'patching' and 'filling gaps' in existing health services patterns. (Godber, 1975.)

The inadequacies of this approach became quickly apparent, especially with the rapid changes in medical care. Often policies regarding desired bed complements would change, new health services would develop or existing services would be required to reorganise in response to conditions which were not known or existent at the time plans for facilities were made. Planned and existing patterns of buildings and locations could not be easily altered to accommodate these types of changes. From the point of adaptability alone, it became clear that planning for health services could no longer be based on isolated considerations of hospital-based services or health centre-based services. Concern for individual buildings had to give way to concern for a range of health services, whose spatial and physical requirements could no longer be determinant factors in planning.

Accompanying this realisation was the expanding understanding of the health-medicine distinction. Health was no longer embodied only in medical care, nor medical care only in hospitals and health centres. This understanding triggered a reappraisal of health services planning, not only where health services provision came under the authority of the state, as in England, but also where planning served only as a nominal regulation of private market provision, as in the United States. Consequently, health services planning changed partially to complement the emerging view of medical care within an ecological definition of health. The focus shifted to a comprehensive outlook, and health services planning assumed a more systematic style.

Planning for 'Need'

The development of comprehensive health services planning was seen as a move 'from an intuitive, spontaneous, and subjective projection of activity based on past experience to a much more deliberate, systematic, and objective process of mobilizing information and organizing resources' (Taylor, 1972, p. 20). This 'intuitive, spontaneous, and subjective' — and often *ad hoc* — approach to health services provision had characterised planning since the late 1940s. It was regarded not so much as a cause of failure as a process which was not capable of keeping pace with the rapidly changing view of health and health care. In the 1960s, an argument emerged among health services observers which held that 'the problem has not been a lack of planning, but the ineffectiveness of the planning that is going on' (Sigmond, 1967, p. 117).

The constraints imposed by existing patterns of health services and the emergence of a comprehensive view of health services contributed importantly to the recognition of a need for change in health services planning, but two other factors influenced the form those changes were to take.

The first of these had to do with the availability of previously unquantified information on health which resulted from studies in epidemiology. With the decline in the incidence of infectious diseases came a decline in the work of epidemiologists who gathered information about the occurrence of such diseases and selected effective action to counteract them. As a result, after the Second World War, underemployed epidemiologists turned their attention firstly to the study of longer term epidemics of chronic disease (such as coronary heart disease) and then to the study of population groups as sufferers of disease. Employing statistical methods, epidemiologists were able to indicate expected incidences of disease for population groups with specific age and sex characteristics.

> The epidemiologist thus became expert at bringing medical statistical knowledge together. It was but a short step to the realisation that almost any health problem involving the counting and categorisation of populations could be considered as his province. Thus, need, demand and delivery of health care were clear candidates for study in the second expansion of the subject, during the mid-1960s. The expectation was that a more thorough understanding of the process of provision of care would enable providers and planners to improve the quality of the services. (Florey and Weddell, 1976, p. 19.)

Information on the health problems of a particular population could be categorised in terms of 'epidemiologic numerators, demographic denominators, and geographic bounds'. By employing this information, health services planners could 'identify the nature and importance of individual health needs, as well as the extent to which these needs are currently translated into demands for health services' (Reinke, 1972, pp. 53–4). Health services, then, could be provided to meet identifiable health needs rather than to fill gaps in existing patterns of facilities. It was argued that planning health services to meet health needs would serve to broaden planners' understanding of medical care in line with the developing ecological view of health (p. 55).

In the late 1950s and early 1960s, it became clear that a wide range of information on population, resources, and need and demand could be made available for use in planning health services (see Bispham *et al.*, 1971 and Bright, 1972). Many problems were associated with this vast quantity of potential data, not least of which was the often unorganised and unreliable state of the data themselves (see Fox, 1973). Further, as far as planning was concerned, epidemiological information could not be regularly employed given the then intuitive and spontaneous state of health services planning. Information produced by epidemiological studies could contribute significantly to health services plans if health services planning techniques could be developed to accommodate it. So, by the mid-1960s, health services planning was being criticised as an activity which had to become more systematic in order to handle the vast bulk of health data effectively and consistently (see, for example, Sigmond, 1967). Some observers suggested the need for health services planning methods which would 'parallel the commonly accepted steps of the scientific method as applied to research' (Taylor, 1972, p. 20).

About the same time that this need for change was being recognised, changes in the planning procedures employed by other planning disciplines opened up a new set of systems techniques for health services planners. Technical and methodological developments in planning, generally, and in town planning and management planning, in particular, constituted a second influence on the form of the operational activities of health services planning from the mid-1960s. Goal-setting, for example, became a formalised activity in the town planning process and, in order to assess the implementation of plans towards established goals, methods for continuous monitoring and evaluation and for information processing were designed to regularise the use of large quantities of data. Health services planning borrowed freely from other branches of what Robinson called the 'family of disciplines and activities which plan and use planning methods'. Health services planning developed into a sequential, if not systematic, set of procedures, much like those employed in town planning. Advocates of the new systems approach to health services provision quickly interjected the established requirements of 'comprehensive planning' in their own field. Health services planning had to be a 'continuous process', 'flexible' to changes in the health environment, 'effective' in meeting the health needs of the population.

Within the framework of these requirements, a series of operational activities has developed to form the health services planning process. Although many have described similar activities to more or less detail (see, for example, Chapman *et al.*, 1977; Taylor, 1972; Dummer, 1973 and Blum, 1974), Dunnell and Holland (1973) identify seven stages of a cyclic work process which broadly and, perhaps, most typically illustrate the activities which health services planners are now seen to do:

1.   Pre-planning — 'the assessment of certain preconditions . . . of which the most important are government interests, legislation, a planning organization, and administrative capacity' . . . the development of information systems and the means to evaluate the results of a plan.
2.   The Ideal — a consideration of the present as well as a general political and social desire for improvement.
3.   Setting Objectives — aim to provide the solution which most nearly achieves the idea . . . Priorities have to be assigned . . .

Alternative methods of achieving objectives should be put forward.

4.   The Plan — setting the targets . . . the most definite and practical part of the process so far. It relates to actual periods and actual changes in services, both policies, and buildings, and represents the planners' choice from several alternatives of the best way to approach the ideal.

5.   Resource Allocation — the planners have to decide how the resources allocated to health can be used to give the best choice between available alternatives so that objectives can be closely approached . . . Required resources of manpower, money and buildings have to be available in the correct quantities and at the correct time during the target period.

6.   Programme — further information is used to develop the decisions about resource allocation into specific building programme and operational policies to ensure that the targets are reached.

7.   Evaluation and Re-assessment — its purpose is to measure the degree to which objectives and targets are fulfilled and also the quality of the results. Evaluation can also lead to re-assessment of the previous decisions and thence to modifications based on the new information gathered. (pp. 252–5.)

These stages do not form a rigid schedule which the health services planner must follow; they do not require the application of specific techniques; nor do they necessarily result in plans of similar comprehensiveness and timing. For example, 'resource allocation', in some cases, may be determined by cost-benefit analyses; in other cases, location and distribution studies may set allocation requirements. 'Plan' and 'Programme', in some cases, may result in long-term master plans; in other cases, plans may comprise short-term, multi-future options. However, Dunnell and Holland's description, although ignoring the detail of various techniques and of resulting plans, illustrates both the range and the limits of what is now commonly seen to be the health services planner's work.

The generally-accepted approach to health services planning may be summarised, then, as predicting future need (or a range of future needs), describing the ways by which those needs may be met, comparing these descriptions with what exists now, and then recommending actions which will change the present pattern of resource allocation to that thought to be required at a future date. Allocation of resources — 'manpower, money and buildings' — comes late in the process and it is this which outwardly distinguishes the new form of health services planning from the old. Health services provision is no longer to be based on buildings. Health services planning, influenced by the emergence of the ecological view of health, by the availability of new forms of epidemiological data and by methodological developments in many planning disciplines, has come to emphasise need for service as the basis for health systems change.[10] 'The objective is to develop a detailed inventory of the services required to meet the health needs of the estimated population of an area at a selected target date.' (Chapman *et al.*, 1977, p. 41.) Only after need for services has been identified are the types, characteristics and timing of the 'resources required to produce those services described'.

The obvious difficulty with this approach, political and financial constraints aside, is: what is need? and who determines it? But this is only one of several problems which arise from the health field to affect the work of health services planners. It is worthwhile to look briefly at some of these difficulties, including the problem of need, if for no other reason than to understand more fully the complicated context within which health services planners do their work.

Comprehensive Health Services Planning: The Problem Areas

The stages of the planning process, outlined above, indicate the many of the factors which bear upon the provision of health services. A number of these factors pose difficulties for planners – difficulties which either arise from the pursuance of a comprehensive approach to health services or continue to confront planners despite the new comprehensive approach. Some of the problems are related specifically to medical services, their production and consumption; others are related to the health field generally. Among the latter group are the distinction between health and medicine, which I have already discussed, and the resultant revolt against medical orthodoxy.

Paradoxes in Medicine

As a consequence of late nineteenth century and early twentieth century improvements in the environmental conditions which affect health, medicine has changed its focus and its effectiveness in preventing premature death. McKeown (1965, p. 61) has identified two main influences which have altered the problems confronting medicine: 'changes in the causes of sickness and disease; and a shift in the age distribution of the population'.

These influences are interrelated. As mortality due to infectious diseases declined, more people survived to suffer diseases which manifest themselves only with longer life.

> In 1970 none of the ten major causes of death were infectious except influenza-pneumonia and certain diseases of early infancy. Today the list is headed by chronic diseases and accidents.
> Chronic diseases also afflict large numbers of the living for long periods of their lives. As health has improved so has the pre-valence of the less tractable forms of disability in later life. (Lalonde, 1974, p. 59.)

For example, in 1900, the average years of life at birth for a white male in the United States was 48; in 1971, the same figure was 68 years. During the same period deaths attributed to diseases of the heart grew from eight per cent to almost forty per cent of all deaths. (Axelrod *et al.*, 1976, pp. 13–18.) Similar patterns have been identified in other industrial countries. Accompanying this trend has been a decline in birth rates, the net effect of which is 'an older population in which diseases associated with ageing are conspicuous' (McKeown, 1976, p. 5).

To these influences must be added changes in technology. Technological change has had a double-edged impact on health services. Technological developments have contributed to environmental and and behavioural conditions which are direct causes of morbidity and mortality. Automobile accidents and industrial cancers are examples. On the other hand, technological change has heightened what Hart called the 'level attained by medical science'. Current diagnostic procedures, for example, are well in advance of what they were only a few years ago. Yet, as some sceptics point out,

> although there have been some real gains (such as pain and other symptom relief, and fertility control), it is clear that many of the most sophisticated contemporary medical procedures are in fact used in attempts to delay death (e.g. cardiac care, various cancer therapies and organ transplants). (Draper *et al.*, 1976, p. 40.)

The effect of these combined influences has been a dramatic increase in the presentation of chronic diseases coincident with the development of specialised procedures and expensive facilities which have little to do with chronic diseases until they become acute. McKeown (1976, p. 6) has summarised this paradox the other way around:

Medicine is now confronted with two very different and, in some respects conflicting trends. One is towards the increased use of technology; the other is towards the predominance of patients who provide little scope for technology, but make large demands for continuing care.

The recognition of the dominance of chronic diseases in industrialised societies and of the need to adjust health services to meet them are not new issues. Preventive medicine directed against behaviourally-induced diseases is receiving increasing political and financial support. Anti-smoking programmes and nutritional advice in popular periodicals are examples of the measures which are being taken to combat the occurrence of chronic disease, under the ecological assumption that the individual is individually responsible for his or her own good health.[11] At the same time, health professionals are pressing for ongoing evaluation of the effectiveness and efficiency of various 'caring' and 'curing' personal medical services (see, for example, Cochrane, 1972) and for a shift in priorities in health services policy and provision to chronic disease prevention and therapy (see, for example, Hetzel, 1974 and Owen, 1976). Other observers suggest the adoption of health-oriented policies in less-'medical' areas of the health field (e.g., housing and transport) as a way to prevent disease and premature death (see Draper *et al.*, 1976).

But the 'challenge to health' within personal health services remains 'to seek an approach which meets and reconciles the needs of technology and care'. This is the challenge which presents itself squarely to the health services planner. High technology facilities and caring facilities impose 'different, and in some respects conflicting', requirements, upon health services plans. McKeown (1976, p. 6) lists some of the hitherto 'largely ignored' planning issues where attention must now be forced: 'the small, uneconomic facility; badly located inadequate sites; inflexible design of buildings; and lack of coordination of the services of a town or region.' But the conflicting trend in health services and in the deployment of resources to accommodate them are not easily or typically resolved within the planner's action space. Politicians and administrators at higher levels within the state's health system hierarchy — whether its authority be exercised through institutionalised state activities or through regulatory legislation — establish policies which filter down to health services planners and, in effect, resolve these types of planning problems, sometimes leaving little discretion open for planning at local levels. In Australia and in Britain, for example, recommendations have been established by national health agencies to guide planning of the functional content and size of hospitals (see Australia, 1974 and Great Britain, 1969). In the United States, specific standards have been established giving legislative priority to the funding of 'primary care services', 'medical group practices', 'studies of nutritional and environmental factors affecting health' and other 'health planning and resource development programs' (United States, 1975). In Canada, concerns with increased costs of health services have led some provinces to actively restrict hospital bed growth and to take a rather complacent view of physician emigration (see Soderstrom, 1978).

The work of those who plan the provision of health services at the point of consumption is often no more than to operationalise such policies at community or regional levels. Nevertheless, some scope for action is seen to exist, wherein the planner plans what services in what quantity is to be provided to whom and where. These decisions are necessarily based on local conditions, and the most significant of these is need for services. Ascertaining need is perhaps the most conspicuous, and certainly one of the most controversial, issues bearing upon the work of the health services planner.

'Demand exists for the concept of need' – Kenneth Boulding

Boulding's (1967, p. 464) statement is not as flippant as it appears on first reading. He explains:

> One demand for a concept of need arises because the concept of demand itself has serious weaknesses and limitations. It assumes away, for instance, a serious epistemological problem. The very idea of autonomous choice implies first that the chooser knows the real alternatives which are open to him, and second that he makes the choice according to value criteria or a utility function which he will not later regret. Both the image of the field of choice and the utility function have a learning problem which, by and large, economists have neglected. This problem is particularly acute in the case of medical care, where the demander is usually a layman faced with professional suppliers who know very much more than he does. The demand for medical care, indeed, is primarily a demand for knowledge or at least the results of knowledge. In the case of ordinary commodities the knowledge that is required is fairly easily available and the market itself is a learning process. If one buys something he does not like he will

not buy it again. In the case of medical care, however, as in the case of certain other commodities such as automobiles, the learning process can easily be fatal (p. 465).

In comprehensive health services planning, where the formal orientation is towards meeting the 'health needs' of the local catchment population, the basis for quantitative provisions is not very firm. Governmentally-imposed ratios of resources to population remain the principal measures for estimation of local requirements for health services. Often justified on the basis of financial constraint and arguments about comparative demand, such ratios rarely have anything to do with patterns of need. But, as Boulding's argument indicates, need is a complex issue and one which, in health services, lacks clear definition. So, in the knowledge that measurements of need are extremely difficult and expensive to make, past utilisation is often employed as an indicator of need. But utilisation is demand, which does not reflect needs which for one reason or another are not presented to the health system; nor does demand expose inappropriate use. Demand for medical and personal health services only reflects market conditions and they may have nothing to do with need for medical care either.

Compare Japan and the United States, for example, whose 'infant mortality rates' and 'average remaining years of life at age 65' are not dissimilar (Axelrod *et al.*, 1976); yet in Japan average length of stay in hospital is more than double that of the United States (Yamamoto and Ohmura, 1975). Indeed, a well-known study examining the utilisation of acute beds in one area of England showed nearly twenty per cent of beds being occupied with no medical or nursing need (Logan *et al.*, 1972); and another study conducted in the United States has shown that for every 100 beds provided in a given catchment area 87 will be utilised regardless of previous inadequacies in health care (Feldstein, 1967). Many studies have cynically concluded 'the appropriate number of beds was the number available' (Australia, 1974, p. 228).

Complicating this already inadequate measure of health services requirements is the problem of where demand originates. Abel-Smith pointed out that demand comes mainly from the doctor, and Boulding illustrates this point to introduce a problematic link between 'demand' and 'need':

One's demand for medical care is what he wants; his need for medical care is what the doctor thinks he ought to have.

The activity originates from the profession rather than from the client, from the supplier rather than from the demander. In its extreme form it takes on the flavor of 'What you need is what I as your professional advisor have to give you; what you want is quite irrelevant' (pp. 465–6).

The physician/provider then translates his assessment of what the patient/consumer needs into a demand for medical services. 'Need is taken to be that which the expert defines as such in any given situation.' (Australia, 1974, p. 224.) And, naturally, reaction to this definition has added fuel to the fiery provider-consumer debate.

Milio (1967, p. 49), for example, suggests that 'expert' definition of the ideal pattern of health 'is influenced by dominant middle-class beliefs, rather than by physiologically-based requirements'. Perceptions of health and illness are influenced by socially- and culturally-bound beliefs and values, as many observers have argued (see, for example, Navarro, 1975; Read, 1966 and Kelman, 1975):

> Someone is gibbering away on his knees, talking to someone who is not there. Yes, he is praying. If one does not accord him the social intelligibility of his behaviour, he can only be seen as mad. (Laing, 1967, quoted in Cox and Mead, 1975, p. 2.)

What a society's health experts define as illness and need clearly depends on what society defines as health.

The lack of appropriate criteria for need and provision of health services complicates the work of health services planners. Questions remain not only with respect to how much of a particular service is appropriate but, just as importantly, with respect to *which* services are appropriate. If need for a given service can not be adequately determined, how can a plan be devised to meet need within a comprehensive and comprehensible framework?

Muddying the Field

Many other issues affect what health services planners do and what they plan. The significance of uneven distribution of health services within a health system is one closely aligned with the criterion of comparative need. Logan (1971), Griffiths (1971) and Navarro (1974a) have discussed the implications of uneven provision of personal medical services on national levels in the UK and US. Cowan (1969) has shown the same problem occurring even within comparatively small urban areas.

Studies of population access to medical services have shown consistently that low-income groups have less contact with physician services than high-income groups (Beck, 1973). Salkever (1975) has shown, in an international study, that this is particularly the case among children of low-income families, at all levels of need. Studies such as these have led Hart (1971a) to formulate what he terms 'the inverse care law: that the availability of good medical care tends to vary inversely with the need of the population served'.

But, for the most part, these continuing debates are seen as peripheral issues, which only indirectly influence the health services planner's work. In order to illustrate what that work is, for the remainder of Part Two, I will discuss the actions taken by planners in two health services planning projects. The geographic bounds for both cases are dominated by new towns, offering a view of the planning work in rapidly developing situations, and thus requiring many planning actions over a short period of time. The case studies are not offered as generalisations of the political-economic concepts discussed earlier, nor as supporting data for later analysis. They are only illustrations of some of the actions which planners take and some of the problems which planners face in the health services planning workplace.

Notes

1.   Dingle notes that the 'medical' factors which did contribute to the decline in tuberculosis mortality were mostly vetinary.

2.   Studies undertaken at the University of Nottingham by Martini and others have shown the sensitivity of outcome indices (in this case, mortality) to medical care and to socio-demographic factors. In their findings, the sensitivity of total mortality to medical care was ·14, as opposed to a sensitivity of ·56 to socio-demographic factors. Corresponding sensitivities of mortality from pneumonia in males between 65 and 75 years of age, as one example, were ·07 and ·78. (Unpublished paper.)

See Draper *et al*. (1977) for a discussion of 'the diverse range of causal — or conditioning — influences that originate in the functioning of the economy' to jeopardise health.

3.   See Salmon (1977) for a discussion of monopoly capital's role in rationalising health services provision.

4.   Navarro (1975) offers an important critique of Illich's view and a well-argued warning to those who may be seduced by the *Medical Nemesis* position.

5.   See Chapter 1.

6.   The further consequences of this collegiate professional control, as Johnson (1972, p. 51) points out, extend beyond the definition of medical requirements:

The social extension of an occupation's authority may be guaged by the degree to which its collective pronouncements on a variety of issues — perhaps only tenuously related to the field of practice — are regarded as authoritative contributions. While the legal and medical associations have been listened to with respect in England on such diverse issues as the economy, juvenile delinquency, drug use and the organization of social welfare, the collective voice of architecture is muted even in areas directly associated with building policy.

Realisation of the influence of these non-biological issues upon health may contribute to an expanding 'ecological' conception of health. However, 'the economy, juvenile delinquency, drug use and the organization of social welfare' also reflect the *range* of issues which the medical profession has been able to bring within the 'jurisdiction' of its professional power relative to the jurisdiction of other professional groups which do not enjoy similar professional power.

7.   Underwood's categories of action space, although useful concepts for an examination of planners' political actions, should not be taken to imply the independence of various planning actions. Roles which the planner would aspire to play (potential action space) can be 'non-actionable' because they are beyond the authority of planning agencies (debated action space); yet, merely by aspiring to those roles, the planner may influence broader problem fields (diffuse action space).

8.   More importantly, the report of the Sankey Commission was to review much of the debate which eventually led to the nationalisation of health services in 1948, although this was never envisaged by the Commission itself.

9.   This point underscores the similarity in health services planning despite differing legislative, financial or administrative structure. Even in Britain, where critics claim the nationalisation of health services 'changed radically the traditional pattern of medical services', as McKeown (1976, p. 1) points out, 'It would be more accurate to say that it [i.e., the NHS] adopted with only minor modification the framework of services which had evolved in the previous century.'

10.   The de-emphasis of physical resources as the bases for plans is not a development unique to health services planning. As goal-setting became an important operational activity in town planning the specificity of physical detail in plans declined. (The Milton Keynes new town plan, discussed in Chapter 1, is a clear demonstration of this change.) The use of 'needs' as parameters within which goals were set was also apparent in a great deal of 'user-needs' research relating to much non-health planning.

11.   Social, economic and political causes for individual behaviour go largely ignored in health prevention programmes. Reasons why people smoke cigarettes, eat 'junk' food and drive fast cars seem to be well known by advertisers, but not by health professionals. Instead of attacking societal causes, preventive medicine tends to blame the victims of illnesses which social conditions induce. For example, trying to correct an individual's food consumption patterns — irrespective of the individual's ability to purchase more nutritional food — 'ignores the enormous power of the economic needs of specific corporate interests in (a) determining that consumption, and (b) stimulating a certain type of production' (Navarro, 1975, p. 369).

Case Study 1

The first example of health services planning which I will present is the plan for the Australian new town of Albury-Wodonga. This example demonstrates some of the types of tasks which health services planners do in their work. At the same time, it casts light on the distinction between planning for need and planning buildings, a distinction around which recent developments in health services planning have centred.

The Albury-Wodonga planning work, which was undertaken between January and August 1975, was an attempt to direct the unified development of a comprehensive range of health services in a rapidly growing area and an area in which health services provision came under the authority of different state agencies.[1]

Albury-Wodonga is a growth centre with an expected expansion from a rural centre of approximately 42,000 inhabitants in 1974 to a large urban area of approximately 300,000 inhabitants by the end of the century. The growth centre actually comprises two towns, Albury and Wodonga, located on opposite sides of the Murray River, which forms part of the boundary between the States of New South Wales and Victoria (see Figure 4.1). New South Wales is responsible for health services planning in Albury and Victoria has similar responsibilities in Wodonga. Of course, dual responsibilities complicate many aspects of the new town's growth. So, in order to avoid possibly contradictory health services development on opposite sides of the Murray River, the health agencies of the two States and of the Australian government, which was a principal financier of Albury-Wodonga development, formed a Health Study Team in January 1975 to undertake an initial planning project for the provision of health services in the new town.

The principal aims of the project were to:

Develop an overall strategy for the development of health services in Albury-Wodonga.

Make recommendations for the provision of physical facilities for health services in the short and medium term.

Make recommendations in relation to the future management of

Figure 4.1: Albury-Wodonga Area Plan

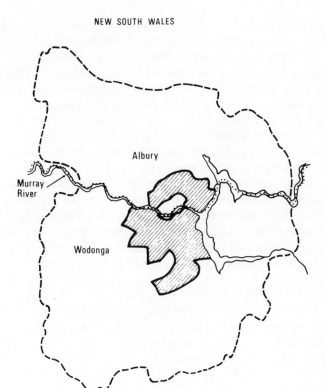

NEW SOUTH WALES

Albury

Murray
River

Wodonga

VICTORIA

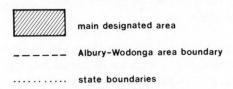

main designated area

Albury-Wodonga area boundary

state boundaries

Source: Albury-Wodonga Development Corporation (1976)

health services in Albury-Wodonga. (Albury-Wodonga Development Corporation — AWDC, 1976, p. 1.)

The Health Study Team worked under the supervision of the Health Planning Team, a group representing New South Wales, Victoria and Australia health agencies and the Albury-Wodonga Development Corporation. The Study Team consisted of two non-medico health services planners from a firm of private planning consultants, a research director of a Victoria health authority and a research officer from the New South Wales Commission. The latter two members, both of whom were physicians, served in part-time capacities. In addition, two other physicians were retained by the Study Team and were consulted during the project.[2]

The health services planning work in Albury-Wodonga followed a series of major phases not dissimilar to the five steps which Robinson cites as the 'model of the rational planning process'.[3] In order to follow the sequence of the Study Team's work and in order to demonstrate the organisation of health services planning work as a process, I will relate the Albury-Wodonga planning project to those five steps.

Step 1: Goal-Setting

Identify the problem or problems to be solved, the needs to be met, the opportunities to be seized upon, and the goals of the community to be pursued, and translate the broad goals into measurable operational criteria.

Problems, Aims and Goals. The Health Study Team began its work by assessing the nature of community health needs, specifically in Australia. After discussions of the changing patterns of health and medicine, the Study Team summarised the 'challenges to health care today' under four headings:

1 — Those problems which remain despite medical advance and which frequently result not in death but in chronic illness; in some cases a principal problem is that the illness is untreatable by the time it presents.
2 — Those problems which have been in a sense exacerbated by the partial success of medical science, resulting in survival of the unfit who consequently require continuing support.
3 — Those problems which are newly important and to a large extent reflect contemporary life-styles in advanced countries, for

example, traffic and other accidents, heart disease and lung cancer.
4 – A group of conditions which are just beginning to be under-
stood and prevented such as abnormalities of reproduction and
diabetes. (AWDC, 1976, p. 20.)

The early work of the Study Team was spent on an assessment of
these challenges and of the health status of Australians generally by
reference to the documentation of community health studies which
had been conducted in Australia. Two of these studies (Krupinski
et al., 1970 and 1971) involved surveys and physical examinations of
an entire population and of sample populations in a rural area and in
an urban area, respectively. A third study (Bridges-Webb, 1971) was
based on records of a general practitioner in a small community and
another was the continuing morbidity survey conducted by the Royal
Australian College of General Practitioners. These studies showed that,
aside from allergic disorders and chronic bronchitis, there was a
relative stability of morbidity patterns between non-Aboriginal
Australian communities.

For Albury-Wodonga, the implication drawn by the Study Team
was that there would not be any likely significant alteration in the
pattern of illness as the new town grew from a rural centre to an urban
centre. On a more general level, the consistency in morbidity patterns
demonstrated by the studies reflected favourably upon the use of the
studies' findings as planning data, given an inability to conduct a
household health survey in Albury-Wodonga. For the Health Study
Team, the data also substantiated the importance of distinguishing
between presented morbidity and needs for medical care, particularly
for psychiatric services, maternal services, and services for the
elderly, for which the studies had shown demand was signficantly
lower than need.

Against this background the Health Study Team defined the
principal aims of health care in any community as:

1. the prevention of illness and disabling abnormality,
2. the identification of illness and disabling abnormality where they
occur,
3. intervention to change the natural history of illness for the better
or to correct abnormality where, in the current state of knowledge,
such intervention is possible, and
4. intervention to alleviate the effects of illness and abnormality.
(AWDC, 1976, p. 24.)

The Health Study Team then 'identified characteristics which, *in its view*, a health care programme should possess in order to be both effective and efficient in the pursuit of these aims' (p. 24. Emphasis added.) The Study Team presented these aims to the Health Planning Team as the basis upon which alternative plans would be evaluated later in the planning process.

The nine characteristics of a health care programme which the Study Team defined were:

1. continuity of care;
2. no duplication of services for the same problem;
3. accessibility — impediments of geographic, legal and social distance are kept to a minimum;
4. resource efficiency — cost efficient in terms of use of both capital and non-capital resources;
5. professional acceptance — health professionals are able to work in conditions acceptable to them;
6. acceptance by the population at large;
7. employment of current medical knowledge;
8. adaptability — the programme is able to respond flexibly to changing needs, attitudes and technology;
9. built-in monitoring — the programme includes mechanisms for evaluating itself over time; this necessitates a continuing monitoring of types of services provided, utilization of services, effectiveness and outcome indices, and changes in the population's state of health. (pp. 24–5.)

These characteristics — from which evaluation criteria or planning goals were later to be adopted — were stated in general terms with no statements regarding specific policy choices. As a consequence, and at the level of the 'measurable operational criteria' which they suggested, the goals were accepted by the supervising Planning Team without controversy.

Medical Strategy. But while the health programme characteristics sought by the Health Study Team were defined broadly, identification of the 'needs to be met' was given more detailed attention. Following the contextual discussions and literature surveys at the beginning of its work, the Study Team attempted to identify a comprehensive range of tasks which are performed within a health system to meet the principal aims of health care:

Medical practice at any one point in time defines a series of *tasks* which are most appropriate to prevent, to identify, to intervene in the progress of or to alleviate the effects of an illness or disabling abnormality. This array of tasks and when they are appropriate may be termed current *medical strategy* for meeting that health problem. (p. 30. Emphasis added.)

The Study Team had argued that 'traditional' health services planning consisted of predicting future needs and describing the best resource allocation by which those needs could be met. As a result, the traditional approach began by considering alternative patterns for the optimal delivery of health services. The consequence of this approach, argued the Study Team, was that an important difference between what the Team termed 'delivery strategy' and 'medical strategy' was often overlooked by early reference to types, sizes and locations of buildings, and confusion and difficulty subsequently resulted from attempts to accommodate health services within defined delivery patterns.

The Health Study Team argued for an alternative approach:

No matter what type of organization of health services is planned for a community, in our view all local health care programmes within the same sphere of medical knowledge and capabilities should offer the served population access to all of the tasks available on the basis of that medical knowledge to meet community health problems. These tasks are given at any one time. They are based on and in fact comprise medical practice within that sphere of medical knowledge and capability. (p. 34.)

By beginning with a consideration of what these community health tasks are, health services planners could avoid problems associated with trying to define optimal health services.

On the basis of these arguments, the Health Study Team identified and defined a comprehensive range of tasks comprised in current medical strategy. Explicitly granting the jurisdiction of medical professionals in this province of health services provision, the Health Study Team solicited advice from medical and health research workers and from 'eminent practitioners' in New South Wales and Victoria regarding current medical practice and developing trends in many health services areas: geriatrics, maternal and child care, psychiatric care, mental retardation, and emergency treatment, among them.

Several meetings were held with the medico members of the Health
Planning Team to further assist in identifying the tasks which compose
the 'medical strategy' specific to the health needs of an Australian
community. After several weeks of work, agreement was reached on
an 'adequate and acceptable' range of health tasks. These tasks were
arrayed in a two-dimensional matrix which was called the Medical
Strategy Matrix and it was to become the foundation for all subsequent work.

The vertical axis of the Medical Strategy Matrix was a classification
of health problems in an Australian community. The Study Team
rejected existing and generally recognised designations of disease
groups — like the International Classification of Disease Codes —
because they suggested only disease-related needs which were not
seen to reflect the full range of community health problems. Instead,
employing techniques used in planning programme budgeting (PPB),
the Study Team defined twenty-one 'missions' of health services in
meeting twenty-one health problems:

> Many tasks [are] undertaken within current medical practice.
> These individual tasks are performed — or operate — to meet a
> particular objective which is the prevention of, the identification of,
> the intervention in the progress of or the alleviation of the effects
> of a particular illness or abnormality. A group or set of tasks, all of
> which operate to meet the same health problem — that is the
> same illness or abnormality — are said to form a single mission.
> All tasks, when considered together, are said to be performing the
> function of the entire health programme, in meeting the needs of a
> defined community. (p. 31.)

The twenty-one missions were grouped into four major community
health problem areas:

1 — Short Term Problems 'the acute, the sub-acute and also the non-
acute problems of a short duration.' Ten missions were grouped in
this area:

- emergency — major trauma
- emergency — minor trauma
- emergency — non-trauma
- medical non-emergency
- surgical non-emergency

•conditions requiring hightly specialised services
•child care
•maternal care
•disorders of the eyes, ears, nose and throat
•dental disorders

2 – Long Term Problems 'chronic continuing medical problems of a population . . . A quite simple age distinction along with a management indication' was used to identify four missions:

•young (i.e. children and adults less than 65 years)
•young with management problems
•aged
•aged with management problems

3 – Mental Health Problems 'distinguished because of their special character and, of course, the special character of the tasks provided to meet them'. Three missions were groups in this area;

•major psychiatric illness
•minor psychiatric illness (distinguishing psychoneuroses, behaviour and personality disorders and transient adjustment reactions)
•alcohol and drug addiction

4 – Problems of the Mentally Retarded 'tasks performed to meet these problems are also operationally distinct.' Four missions were grouped in this area, based on clinical classifications:

•profoundly retarded
•severely retarded
•moderately retarded
•mildly retarded (p. 32.)

Forming the horizontal axis of the Medical Strategy Matrix were classifications of health tasks. Six broad classification parameters were developed, subdividing tasks by resource requirements or specifications into ten groups.

The principal classification of all tasks, *time of intervention*, distinguished between those tasks performed to intervene in the natural course of a health problem before it manifests itself and those tasks performed after the problem manifests itself. Tasks performed 'before manifestation' were subdivided, by a second classification, *nature of task*, into those oriented towards presymptomatic 'detection' of health problems and those oriented towards 'avoidance' or prevention of health problems.

Tasks performed 'after manifestation' were further subdivided by four classification groups. *Locational implications* distinguished between those tasks whose performance entailed a 'specialised support environment' and those which could entail a 'home' environment. Tasks requiring 'specialised support environment' were distinguished by *duration of task*: 'uninterrupted', 'sessional' or 'consultative'. The 'uninterrupted' tasks were classified by *urgency*: 'crisis control', 'high dependency' or 'low dependency'; the 'consultative' tasks were classified by *health professional involved*: 'specialised practitioner', 'community practitioner' or 'allied health'.

Within the cells of the matrix the Study Team listed the 'health tasks which should be undertaken to meet those [community health] problems, on the basis of authoritative advice as to best contemporary practice' (p. 31). These tasks were labelled 'not to identify every specific activity, but rather to identify the types of tasks required to meet each health problem' (p. 22). Some of the 210 cells were empty, indicating that no task was recognised as required of a specific community health classification to meet, 'adequately and acceptably', a specific mission; other cells had more than one task. For example, there was no task listed under the locational classification 'home' ('after manifestation') for dental disorders; under the urgency classification 'low dependency', ('uninterrupted', 'specialised support environment', 'after manifestation') four tasks − convalescence, major diagnostic investigation, minor diagnostic investigation, and rehabilitation − were listed for the surgical non-emergency mission. Altogether, over 200 tasks were identified as composing current medical strategy for an Australian community.

The Medical Strategy Matrix was seen as a summary of the outstanding tasks of a community health care programme. It could be used, the Study Team argued, as a baseline from which health services planners could monitor future changes in health tasks which would influence health services delivery. More importantly, it would assist planners by identifying the comprehensive range of tasks which must be considered in planning health services for a community. The adoption of this alternative approach to health services planning was, in the view of the Study Team, a departure from the logic comprising much current health services planning. It recognises that there is a specific and identifiable body of medical knowledge and capabilities and that the proper role of planning is to ensure that the entire body of that same medical knowledge and capability is available within the community health care programme, the organisation of which planning means to effect. (p. 34.)

The Study Team argued, in line with this view, that as health services planning moved from considerations of 'medical strategy' to considerations of 'delivery strategy' the 'knowledge' and 'capabilities' required would be less that of the 'medico' and more that of the 'planner'.

Step 2: Plan-Formulation

Design alternative solutions or courses of action (plans, policies, programs) to solve the problems and/or fulfill the needs, opportunities, or goals, and predict the consequences and effectiveness of each alternative.

The health tasks which made up medical strategy were the operators by which the health problems in Albury-Wodonga were to be met. The many ways in which tasks could be grouped and distributed within the new town formed alternative delivery strategies. The Health Study Team defined *comprehensive health services delivery strategy* as a specific way of organising all of the health tasks of medical strategy. Within the comprehensive delivery strategy, smaller groupings of tasks were labelled 'services'. Alternative delivery strategies for each of the various services could be designed and evaluated relatively independently of delivery strategies for other services. In this way, strategies for the delivery of different services could be organised differently, within a comprehensive delivery strategy, should plan evaluation prove this to be most appropriate.

Interdependency of Plan Tasks. The Health Study Team argued that some tasks in medical strategy are interdependent and that any 'delivery strategy which separates tasks which are interdependent could obstruct if not prevent the delivery of effective and efficient health care' (p. 35). As a result of this view and before developing alternative delivery strategies, the Study Team undertook 'a lengthy task-by-task analysis . . . to produce an interdependency matrix' (p. 36).

The intent was to identify those tasks which are to be located in association with each other, as intact 'service' groups, in order to achieve effective and efficient performance of all of those tasks, irrespective of the pattern of health care delivery.

Once again advice was solicited from health researchers and practitioners; the Study Team also consulted reports and documents of Australian, Victorian and New South Wales health authorities. Four criteria were employed to identify task interdependencies:

A — two or more tasks requiring 'skills acquired during the same professional training' or 'the same facilities or supporting services (for example, daycare rehabilitation for all kinds of physical disability)';

B — two or more tasks which 'authoritative opinion requires be performed in close physical association to avoid harm or to gain effectiveness (for example, obstetric and neonatal care)';

C — two or more tasks 'which require participation of the same professional groups of workers or which can share facilities . . . and which would be impractically difficult to form into separate organisationally and economically viable units (for example, medical investigations and surgical procedures)'; and

D — tasks which 'would be impractically difficult to form into organisationally and economically viable units' if performed in a location separate from tasks 'within the same clinical discipline requiring more highly specialized skills and services . . . (for example, minor medical investigations)'. (pp. 35–6.)

Detailed analysis of each task, citing argument for association with other tasks, where appropriate, allowed the Study Team to show whether interdependencies were based on involvement of the same health professionals (criterion A), or physical facility requirements (criteria B, C or D), or on both (criteria A and B, C or D). Approximately seventy per cent of all tasks were shown to be locationally interdependent with one or more other tasks, thus forming many service groups, each of which related to one or more missions of medical strategy. The Study Team argued that 'although these service groups can be expanded on the basis of planning organisation to include other tasks [with which they are not interdependent] they cannot be sensibly divided' (p. 36). The interdependent service groups were indivisible units within various health delivery strategies.

Before designing alternative delivery strategies, the Health Study Team conducted a cluster analysis of the task interdependency to identify principal service groups which could be used as the cores of delivery strategies. This cluster analysis entailed a subdivision of the tasks by the twenty-one mission classifications. The dependency of each group of tasks related to the same mission to each other group of tasks related to other missions was identified. It was shown that there were five main groups of services, related to five sets of missions, which were entirely or largely independent of each other. The Study Team then employed these major groups of tasks, or 'major services', as the basis for the organisation of five different sets of alternative delivery strategies. One of each of these five types of delivery strategy would be selected as part of a comprehensive delivery strategy.

Alternative Delivery Strategies.   The five types of delivery strategy were:

1 — Episodic Illness and Injury Services — comprised of all tasks related to the medical non-emergency and surgical non-emergency missions and all other interdependently associated tasks.

2 — Maternal Care Services — comprised of all tasks related to the maternal care mission and all other interdependently associated tasks.

3 — Aged Chronic Condition Services — comprised of all tasks related to the aged and the aged with management problems missions and all other interdependently associated tasks.

4 — Psychiatric Illness Services — comprised of all tasks related to major psychiatric illness and minor psychiatric illness missions and all other interdependently associated tasks.

5 — Mental Retardation Services — comprised of all tasks related to the profoundly retarded, the severely retarded, the moderately retarded and the mildly retarded missions and all other inter-dependently associated tasks. (pp. 36—7.)

The Health Study Team argued that many variables could be employed as the framework for delivery strategies. However, because it saw 'the main purpose' of its work as 'the management of investment in facilities' required to accommodate health tasks, the Study Team elected to vary the organisation of health services for the five different types of strategy 'on the basis of a relative scale of centralisation of services, which principally determines the pattern of facilities required'. This resultant range of alternative delivery strategies would enable the Study Team 'to identify a range of different directions' in which facilities investments could be made. (p. 37.)

Eighteen alternative delivery strategies were designed:

> This number is not exhaustive. The delivery strategies . . . are intended to represent those organisational patterns which entail a significant difference in forms of facilities implications. (p. 38.)

For each of the five different types of delivery strategy the range of organisational patterns extended from the 'highly concentrated' to the 'highly decentralised'. Episodic Illness and Injury Services and Maternal Care Services were organised in three alternative strategies each; four alternatives were developed for the delivery of the other three service groups. Each delivery strategy included all of the tasks related to the major 'largely independent' mission or missions of that type, plus all associated interdependent tasks or groups of tasks. No strategy entailed a separation of tasks which formed indivisible groups.

Maternal Care Services, for example, comprised 'all tasks related to the maternal care mission and all other interdependent tasks'. Within the maternal care mission, the Study Team had identified sixteen tasks which were classified and numbered upon the Medical Strategy Matrix in this way (tasks are in italics):

after manifestation:
    specialised support environment:
        uninterrupted:
            crisis control:
                54 – abnormal delivery
            high dependency:
                55 – normal delivery
            low dependency:
                56A – pre-natal admission
                56B – post-natal admission

sessional:
> 57A – *pre-natal services*
> 57B – *mothercraft*

consultative:
> specialist practitioner:
> > 58 – *diagnosis and clinical management*
>
> community practitioner:
> > 59 – *diagnosis and clinical measurement*
>
> allied health:
> > 60 – *pre-natal and post-natal physiotherapy and social counselling*

home environment:
> 61A – *follow-up care*
> 61B – *household support: assist in tasks of daily living*

before manifestation:
> detection:
> > 62A – *ante-natal examination*
> > 62B – *post-natal examination*
>
> avoidance:
> > 63A – *health education*
> > 63B – *immunisation*
> > 63C – *family planning*

The first of the three alternative delivery strategies for Maternal Care Services reflected a 'highly centralised' organisation:

> This strategy envisaged centres of obstetric and neo-natal care which bring together normal and abnormal deliveries, where the patient may be under the care of a specialist or community practitioner, and care of normal and abnormal neonates, with pre-natal day care and mothercraft programmes, and serves as a base for domiciliary services. Specialist consultative services and consultative services offered by members of allied health professions are accommodated within the centre, or in the case of private practice may be offered independently.
>
> Consultative services offered by community practitioners are accommodated separately. (p. 45.)

All tasks related to the maternal care mission, with the exception of community practitioner task (number 59) and immunisation (number

63B) were grouped together in this strategy. Eight other tasks were shown, through the interdependency analysis, to require locational association with the tasks of this large group. For example, the crisis control task related to the child care mission was identified as interdependent with the abnormal delivery task of the maternal care mission (number 54) because 'authoritative opinion' required that foetal intensive care units be established within larger obstetric units. These eight associated tasks were included in this highly centralised maternal care service group. The specialist practitioner task (number 58) composed a second independent group in this strategy, but one which, as the Study Team explained, may be accommodated with the central service group or independently. Sixteen other tasks, all related to other missions and all classified to the community practitioner, formed the associated services within the third group in this strategy, which was based upon tasks number 59 and 63B.

A 'moderately decentralised delivery strategy' was the second alternative organisation for Maternal Care Services:

This strategy envisages comprehensive obstetric units dealing with all deliveries, whether normal or abnormal, and where the patient may be under the care of a specialist or a community practitioner. Such units will also provide facilities for pre-natal admissions, ante- and post-natal examinations and for the care of both normal and abnormal neonates.

A separate organisation and location is envisaged for pre-natal day care and mothercraft programmes, consultative services by members of allied health professions, more specialised domiciliary services and family planning programmes.

The third tier of the system is formed by consultative services offered by community practitioners with some domiciliary services

Specialist consultative services may be provided in association with either the obstetric unit, the day care facility or independently. (p. 47.)

In this delivery strategy the large group of tasks presented in the first strategy was divided into two groups. All tasks requiring an uninterrupted time duration (numbers 54, 55, 56A and 56B) and all detection tasks (numbers 62A and 62B) were maintained in a central group. Two of the original eight associated tasks, both relating to the child care mission, were also included in this service group. Sessional tasks (numbers 57A and 57B), the allied health task (number 60), home environment tasks (numbers 61A and 61B), and two of the three avoidance tasks (numbers 63A and 63C) formed a separate service group in the 'moderately decentralised' Maternal Care Services delivery strategy. Six interdependent tasks, all classified as home environment, were associated with this second service group. Once again, the specialist practitioner task (number 58) was grouped separately, with possible links to either the first or second group indicated in the strategy. The fourth group of tasks — what the Study Team had called the 'third tier' (due to the non-'tiered' nature of the specialist practitioner group) — comprised the community practitioner task (number 59) and immunisation (number 63B), plus the sixteen associated community practitioner tasks.

The third alternative delivery strategy which the Health Study Team designed for Maternal Care Services was characterised by a 'highly decentralised' organisation:

This strategy envisages specialist obstetric units for abnormal deliveries, under the care of a specialist, with facilities for neonatal intensive care, the care of premature babies, and ante- and post-natal examinations.

Specialist consultative services may be offered from the specialist obstetric unit, or in the case of private practice, independently.

Normal deliveries, pre-natal day care and mothercraft programmes, consultative services by members of allied health professions, ante- and post-natal examinations, more specialised domiciliary services and family planning programmes are accommodated in peripheral institutions.

The third tier of the system is formed by consultative services offered by community practitioners together with some domiciliary services. (p. 49.)

In this strategy the high dependency normal delivery task (number 55) was separated from all other uninterrupted time duration tasks and grouped with sessional tasks (numbers 57A and 57B), the allied health task (number 60), home environment tasks (numbers 61A and 61B), and the two avoidance tasks (numbers 63A and 63C) which constituted the second service group in the 'moderately decentralised' delivery strategy. This left the crisis control task (number 54) and the low dependency tasks (number 56A and 56B) as the three uninterrupted time duration tasks forming the specialist obstetric units. In addition, the detection tasks, ante- and post-natal examination (numbers 62A and 62B), were included in both of the service groups to ensure the capability of their being undertaken with all obstetric procedures. These differences did not alter the groupings of associated services. The specialist practitioner service group and the community practitioner/avoidance service group were similar to those in the 'highly centralised' and 'moderately decentralised' delivery strategies.

The organisational differences of the principal tasks in each of the three delivery strategies for Maternal Care Services can be summarised numerically by the task numbers above. The 'highly centralised' strategy comprised three service groups:

• group 1 – tasks 54, 55, 56A, 56B, 57A, 57B, 60, 61A, 62A, 62B, 63A and 63C,
• group 2 – task 58,
• group 3 – tasks 59 and 63B.

The 'moderately decentralised' strategy comprised four groups:

• group 1 – tasks 54, 55, 56A, 56B, 62A and 62B,
• group 2 – task 58,
• group 3 – tasks 57A, 57B, 60, 61A, 61B, 63A and 63C,
• group 4 – tasks 59 and 63B.

And the 'highly decentralised' strategy also comprised four groups:

• group 1 – tasks 54, 56A, 56B, 62A and 62B,
• group 2 – task 58,
• group 3 – tasks 55, 57A, 57B, 60, 61A, 61B, 62A, 62B, 63A and 63C,
• group 4 – tasks 59 and 63B.

The Health Study Team designed a similar range of alternative delivery strategies for each of the four other types: Episodic Illness and Injury Services, Aged Chronic Condition Services, Psychiatric Services and Mental Retardation Services. Because the delivery strategies were based on the comprehensive range of tasks identified as medical strategy, the Study Team argued that

> any combination [of] strategies for each service, when considered together with the other independent tasks, and services, could serve as a comprehensive delivery strategy for all health tasks of the

Medical Strategy Matrix. (p. 38.)

Any of the many combinations of strategies possible, therefore, could serve as a pattern for the delivery of health services and operationalise 'the function of the entire health programme, in meeting the needs of a defined community'.

Step 3: Plan-Evaluation

Compare and evaluate the alternatives with each other and with the predicted consequences of unplanned development, and choose, or help the decision maker or decision-making body to choose, that alternative whose probable consequences would be preferable.

Health Services for Albury-Wodonga. The next stage of planning work undertaken by the Study Team was the evaluation of the five types of alternative strategy to select that one from each type which would be expected to achieve the desired characteristics of a health care programme in Albury-Wodonga. The objectives sought in town planning development of the Albury-Wodonga new town were reviewed, as were the alternative growth strategies which had been put forward by the town planners. In this phase the health services planners worked with the town planning consultants to obtain data and projections of demographic and social characteristics of the expected population.

Demographic projections were studied. Low and high growth rates would present different levels of need for health services, and these would have to be taken into account in the implementation stage of health services planning.

Other factors relating to the new town's growth were investigated in preparation for evaluation. For example, one of the goals which had been employed in the town design was 'flexibility'. The stated intent of the town plan was to commit future investments in the growth centre for only a short term, and to keep open many options from which future residents and future planners could elect future, longer-term, development patterns. This amplified the uncertainties which normally affect health services planning. In this context, questions regarding the direction in which Albury-Wodonga's future growth would begin — north in Albury or south in Wodonga — posed uncertainties relating to the balance of health services distribution, not only geographically, but also within the joint responsibility of the two States' health authorities.

Two other factors arising from the plan for the rapid growth of

Albury-Wodonga were seen to 'significantly affect the requirements for the distribution of health services':

1   On the basis of migration pattern projection, the age distribution of the population of Albury-Wodonga is expected to become increasingly skewed toward the younger age groups as growth continues.

2   The growth of Albury-Wodonga will result in a geographic distribution of the population over a much wider area than at present. The Thurgoona [northeast of Albury] and Middle Creek [southeast of Wodonga] centres as planned are located approximately 25 kilometers apart via the existing Albury and Wodonga centres. These distances pose particular difficulties when considering the trade-offs between centralisation of some services for economy and decentralisation of those services for accessibility. (p. 83.)

Within these local conditions and constraints, the Health Study Team evaluated the alternative delivery strategies for application to Albury-Wodonga.

Evaluation of Alternative Delivery Strategies. The criteria which the Study Team employed to evaluate each of the eighteen alternative delivery strategies were derived from the nine characteristics of an effective and efficient health care programme, which had been established in the early stages of the planning work. The Health Study Team categorised the nine characteristics into four sets of criteria. The 'broadly' phrased characteristics were elaborated upon with some less-generalised detail.

The first set of criteria included three characteristics which 'related to patient care'. *Continuity of care* was explained as entailing two aspects, continuity of care for the patient within one episode of illness and continuity of care as surveillance for a whole family over a long period. *Accessibility* was viewed as 'important because impediments to medical care [knowledge, attitudes, languages, money, and social and geographic distance] inevitably impede its effectiveness'. *Current medical knowledge* not only sought to meet changing patterns of disease, particularly the rise of chronic disease, but also sought to avoid iatrogenic disease which becomes more prevalent as medical science becomes 'more powerful and therefore considerably more dangerous' (p. 85).

Three characteristics 'related to use of resources' formed the second set of criteria. *No duplication of services* was seen to promote efficiency (and, by aiding continuity of care, effectiveness). *Resource efficiency* was explained as achieving medical effectiveness, on the one hand, and cost effectiveness on the other. The latter was considered in terms of both capital and operating expenditures. *Adaptability* emphasised the need for the health care programme in Albury-Wodonga to be able to change should future conditions warrant (p. 85).

Built-in monitoring formed a set of its own, labelled 'internal audit'. The Study Team explained that strategies should be evaluated against this criterion to assess whether or not they would facilitate the achievement of 'a continuing review of the health of a total population sample, offering, in addition to information about patients, a data base which deals with all needs both met and unmet by the health services' (p. 86).

Professional acceptance and *acceptance by the population-at-large* were categorised as the 'local acceptance' criteria set.

The Health Study Team did not view the several criteria as independent; many were interrelated. *No duplication of services*, for example, affected *continuity of care*, and the 'patient care criteria' were dependent upon *built-in monitoring* and *adaptability*. The evaluation which the Study Team undertook, however, weighed each of the delivery strategies against each of the criteria separately.

Here the relative independence of the Study Team from the Planning Team became important. The Study Team explained that the process of evaluating the alternative delivery strategies sought to answer the question 'How far does this particular strategy help to achieve each of the health care programme characteristics?' (p. 88). The evaluation process was openly subjective. In this regard, the Study Team was clear, explaining subsequently to the Health Planning Team that a study team differently constituted could well have answered the evaluation question differently and could have recommended different strategies as a result.[4]

The Study Team explained its evaluation as a 'consensus method'. A three point scale was employed, through which each strategy was 'described with confidence' as 'facilitating', 'constraining', or 'neither facilitating nor constraining' achievement of each health programme characteristic. In the evaluation 'no assumptions were made about the relative importance of the characteristics . . . equal weighting' was employed (p. 88).

Lengthy descriptions of the evaluation discussions of the Health

Study Team were reported in the Technical Supplement to the health services plan. There is no need to detail that discussion here. Instead, excerpts from the abbreviated evaluation discussion for Maternal Care Services, which were included in the main report, will suffice as an example of the Study Team's work.

Patient Care

The constraint on access presented by a highly centralised strategy was perceived as particularly important in the case of maternal care services. The separation of facilities for normal and abnormal deliveries, and concomitant absence of neonatal intensive care facilities for deliveries expected to be normal, as required by a highly decentralised strategy, incurs particular risks in terms of perinatal morbidity and child damage. A small proportion of abnormal deliveries can be anticipated despite excellent antenatal care and minor errors in the management of reproductive performance can result in handicapped life. On the other hand continuity of care may in this case be facilitated by a highly decentralised strategy, since normal pregnancies can be managed throughout from the peripheral unit.

Resource Use

A highly centralised strategy facilitates economic resource use in terms of specialised facilities and equipment, as well as in terms of the use of skilled personnel. Both decentralised strategies incur operating cost penalties because of the separation of tasks requiring the same skilled personnel. A highly decentralised strategy entails duplication of facilities and equipment, and would be difficult to reverse in future both in terms of discarding or finding alternative uses for specialised facilities, and in terms of changing patterns of utilisation.

Internal Audit

A moderately decentralised strategy, because it entails a separation of tasks related to antenatal care, delivery and postnatal care between different location, poses more difficulties in achieving effective information systems than either a highly centralised or highly decentralised strategy.

Local Acceptance Criteria

Local health professionals indicated a strong preference for a maternal care services organisation which would allow community practitioners easy access to obstetric units for normal deliveries and consequently for a highly decentralised organisation. In the light of no strong indication of preference from the community at large in Albury-Wodonga, all strategies were scaled equally in regard to population acceptance.

Evaluation Summary

A highly decentralised delivery strategy for maternal care services is least preferred. A highly centralised strategy emerges as narrowly preferred to a moderately centralised strategy. Only a moderately decentralised strategy, however, meets all evaluation criteria without posing some constraint: A highly centralised strategy constrains achievement of accessibility. A highly decentralised strategy constrains achievement of resource efficiency, no duplication of services and adaptability. (pp. 90—1.)

Selection of Preferred Comprehensive Strategy. From the 'consensus evaluation' process, one delivery strategy from each of the five types emerged as facilitating the achievement of all the criteria better than others:

- the moderately decentralised Episodic Illness and Injury strategy,
- the highly centralised Maternal Care strategy,
- the highly decentralised Aged Chronic Condition strategy,
- the moderately decentralised Psychiatric Illness strategy, and
- the moderately decentralised Mental Retardation strategy.

Before selecting those strategies which were preferred for inclusion in a comprehensive health services delivery strategy, however, the Study Team employed sensitivity analysis techniques to test the 'sensitivity of each strategy against possible future changes' in priorities which were given to criteria sets and in development patterns in Albury-Wodonga.

This sensitivity analysis demonstrated that only in extreme circumstances — for example, emphasis on the importance of one criteria set being tripled or quadrupled relative to that of others — would a change in preferred delivery strategy be warranted for four of the five strategy types. For the Maternal Care Services, however, where a highly centralised strategy had emerged from consensus evaluation as 'narrowly preferred', the Study Team found that 'an increase in emphasis on patient care by a factor of two warrants a change in preference to a moderately decentralised strategy' (p. 97). Furthermore, the sensitivity analysis showed that should a southern option for directed growth in Albury-Wodonga (adjacent to Wodonga) be elected by the town planners, the highly centralised Maternal Care Services strategy would be preferred by an even narrower margin than first guaged, due to the constraints imposed on accessibility from the resulting population distribution.[5]

The Health Study Team argued its own preference for an increased emphasis on the importance of patient care criteria and this argument, compounded by the fact that the 'moderately decentralised' Maternal Care delivery strategy did not constrain achievement of any of the evaluation criteria, led the Study Team to recommend a delivery strategy organisation other than that which emerged from the consensus evaluation. So, while the strategies which emerged from the other four types as best facilitating the achievement of the evaluation criteria were maintained within the preferred comprehensive delivery strategy, the Study Team proposed a moderately decentralised strategy for the delivery of Maternal Care Services.

The five types of service delivery strategy were combined by the Health Study Team with the independent tasks to form the strategic comprehensive health services delivery strategy for Albury-Wodonga.

In summary the core of the comprehensive health services delivery is characterised by:

Comprehensive institutions embracing both specialist and non-specialist services providing inpatient services for episodic illness and injury and maternal care.

A pattern of dispersed services and institutions, each dedicated to meeting specific kinds of problems arising among aged suffering from chronic conditions.

A pattern of psychiatric inpatient services which brings together in a single unit early treatment, rehabilitation and long term care of the chronically ill.

Accommodation for the severely and profoundly retarded separate from hostel accommodation provided for the moderately and mildly retarded.

Centres for day care programmes, and domiciliary services, also providing consultative facilities for allied health professions together with some specialists.

Organisation of some domiciliary services, notably community

nurses and home helps in association with community
practitioners. (pp. 100–1.)

Step 4: Plan-Implementation

Develop a plan of action for effectuating or implementing the
alternative selected, including budgets, project schedules, regulatory
measures, and the like.

The Health Study Team maintained that until this stage the health
services planning approach which it had employed was 'facility-free' —
that is, free of any considerations of types, sizes or locations of
buildings. A preferred comprehensive delivery strategy for Albury-
Wodonga was regarded as a strategic framework within which decisions
relating to these considerations could be taken:

> The principal purpose of the preferred comprehensive health
> services strategy is to provide direction for the broad range of
> health services development in the Albury-Wodonga growth
> centre. It is not a plan for facilities. It is, rather, a guide for
> facilities planning . . .
>   Decisions will need to be taken over the longer term to continue
> development of health services in keeping with the preferred com-
> prehensive delivery strategy. New information regarding the assess-
> ment of need may significantly alter projections made now of
> service requirements in the longer term. As new information
> becomes available, either because it was not known or available
> before or because old information takes a new and revised form,
> old decisions need to be evaluated and if appropriate new
> decisions need to be made. (p. 126.)

Indeed, the Health Study Team argued that the direction of the comprehensive delivery strategy itself may need alteration over time. This
was one of the reasons why the Study Team had documented in detail
the methodology it had employed in planning, so that 'subjective
decisions' could be exposed to re-evaluation as future conditions might
warrant.

For the 'short term' and 'medium term' future of the new town
(these being time periods related to population growth and employed
throughout the Development Corporation plans), the Study Team
employed their recommended health services delivery strategy to develop
proposals for the provision of health services and facilities. This is where

the first explicit decisions about building types and sizes and locations were taken in the planning process.

The foundation for all of these decisions was the comprehensive health services delivery strategy. Each of the groups of tasks which made up the preferred strategy types served as a sort of functional brief for a health services facility. For example, the first service group of the Maternal Care Service strategy would be accommodated in a facility whose functional content would be abnormal and normal delivery (obstetric) tasks, pre-natal admission, post-natal convalescence, and ante- and post-natal examination.

The Health Study Team considered all service groups within the comprehensive delivery strategy to ascertain groups which should or could share a common location. Some groups, for example those which included community practitioner services, were linked via common associated tasks. Other groups which were not required in great quantity for the early population numbers, such as those which included psychiatric tasks of an uninterrupted nature, were locationally grouped with other medical tasks of the same nature over the short and medium term.

An important factor in these considerations, as the last example demonstrates, was the size of the units or services required for different levels of population. Here, the Health Study Team turned again to demographic projections, including one of its own. The Study Team also assessed the minimum 'viable unit' for each major service element. 'Viable units' were defined as 'the minimum desirable provision of a quantifiable building element, to ensure effective and efficient delivery of a particular health service' (p. 110). Data on existing provision of health services in Albury and in Wodonga, which had been gathered from available data and from its own surveys, were also reviewed by the Study Team.

In addition to this information, the Study Team employed published criteria for the provision of services emerging from government agencies or 'expert advice' — all of which the Study Team reviewed, particularly where ratios of resource provision to population size varied between different sources. From these, the Study Team recommended quantitative provision for each of the health service groups both for the short term (as the population grew to 60,000 persons) and for the medium term (as the population grew to 96,000 persons).

The Study Team made two qualifications upon these quantitative recommendations:

1. We relied on available information [relating to population ratios of services provision] since the scope of the study did not contemplate mounting substantial basic research. While at first sight this may seem a defect in the study, this is not necessarily the case. First a great deal of information and research is in fact available which should be fully exploited before embarking on 'ad-hoc' studies. Second, if health planning for geographical areas is to become a routine feature of the management of health services in Australia, it must be possible to devise adequate plans without incurring very large costs and delaying necessary decisions each time a plan is proposed by embarking on major research work.
2. From a planning point of view, the assessment of need only has to be as good as is necessary to make the planning decisions required by this study. From the outset our intention has been to ensure provision of adequate and accepted minimal health standards not optimal standards. Furthermore, Albury-Wodonga will remain a relatively small community in the short and medium term. Consequently minor adjustments to quantitative criteria for provision of services will not significantly alter the scope of investments which have been made. (pp. 124—5.)

By employing such criteria the Study Team argued in support of the use of comparative need to assess requirements for health services provision.

With the specification for additional health services provision (over existing services) made, the Health Study Team employed location planning techniques and decision analysis to recommend short- and medium-term construction and location of health services facilities. New facilities for existing hospitals in Albury-Wodonga were also recommended.

The distribution of health services between the several facilities was derived directly from the comprehensive health services delivery strategy. Briefly, in terms of buildings, the short- and medium-term plan envisaged the provision of new accommodation for additional medical, surgical, obstetric, paediatric, psychiatric and other inpatient services. The accommodation was to take the form of a hospital located in Middle Creek (southeast of Wodonga). Additional facilities were to be added to existing hospitals in Albury and Wodonga to accommodate additional services in the short term or to remedy existing deficiencies.

The core of the health services plan was a series of community day

care and consultative facilities, operated on three tiers. The Local
Support Centre, serving a population of approximately 10,000 persons,
would accommodate medical and dental consultative services, community
nursing, home helps, and baby health and child care services, among
others. As a local area grew to approximately 30,000 persons the
Local Support Centre could be upgraded or supplemented with a
Community Support Centre which offered accommodation for
additional services, such as allied health professionals and domiciliary
programmes. The primary health service contact point, however, particularly over the short term was to be accommodated in 'outposts',
located in localities most removed from the main centre, providing
community practitioner services and child care nursing.

Nursing homes and hostels for care of the aged, separated by
dependency requirements, were also recommended. Training centres,
multi-diagnostic workshops, psychiatric hostels, transport and ambulance services and other facilities were recommended to accommodate
the range of tasks which had been identified in the Medical Strategy
Matrix and grouped according to the preferred comprehensive delivery
strategy.

Step 5: Plan-Review and Feedback

Maintain the plan on a current and up-to-date basis, based on feedback and review of information to adjust steps 1 through 4 above.

The Health Study Team viewed its planning approach as one which
avoided 'making decisions where there is no immediate pressure to
commit resources', thereby preserving the Development Corporation's
goal of 'flexibility' (p. 145).

This approach, the Study Team argued, required 'continuing planning,
monitoring, evaluation, and innovation' in order to preserve the comprehensive view of health services provision in Albury-Wodonga. In
order to assist this continuing planning commitment beyond its own
work, the Study Team recommended a health services planning and
management programme.

A 'health planning organisation' was proposed which would continue
under the supervision and direction of the existing Health Planning
Team. However, day-by-day planning would be undertaken by a Joint
Health Services Co-ordination Committee. This Committee would
bring together 'representatives of each of the Hospital Boards in
Albury-Wodonga, managers of the services directly provided by the
State Governments and representatives of the principal voluntary

organisations concerned with health services' (p. 147).

The Study Team recommended that responsibility for the planned development 'of integrated programmes of care for major groups of health problems arising in the community' be invested in a series of 'task forces' under the auspices of the Joint Health Services Co-ordinating Committee. The work of these task forces would be related to particular missions (or groups of missions) of the Medical Strategy Matrix: child care services, for example, or psychiatric services. Membership of each task force would be composed of professional health workers with responsibilities or interests in the concerned services. These bodies would not only plan continued provision of health services but also review changes in medical strategy and in the information upon which strategic decisions had been taken in order to alter the direction of provision if required.

In its recommendations for a continued health services planning organisation, the Study Team proposed that members of the community participate as two separate bodies: the first consisting of 'members of the public, who do not derive their professional livelihood from the provision of health services, and who might be elected at a public meeting', the second consisting of members nominated by 'professional associations in the area . . . on a quota basis'.[6]

Finally, the Study Team recommended a 'Review and Evaluation Group' be established to expose the continuing planning work 'to periodic critiques, insights and recommendations of health services planners not directly associated with the day-to-day activities of the health care system or its planning and management' (p. 150). This group was to be composed of 'some of the most distinguished Australian researchers into the organisation of medical care'.

To initiate the 'innovation' work of the Albury-Wodonga Health Planning Organisation, the Health Study Team ended its report by proposing the establishment of the 'Albury-Wodonga Project'. Briefly, this consisted of four 'test' programmes which might be undertaken in Albury-Wodonga:

> a community health survey to serve as a basis for continued family health studies in order to assess effectiveness of the health services programme;
>
> the designation of one of the Community Support Centres as a research and development centre where investigations on such issues as new roles for medical professionals, new information systems, and the use of traditionally 'hospital-based' services such as laboratories

could be undertaken;

possibly linked to this research and development centre, a pilot health maintenance programme, serving a registered population and operated within the Australian Government's newly nationalized health insurance scheme; and

in keeping with the 'internal audit' evaluation criterion, a comprehensive information, survey and record linkage system which would study types of services provided, utilization, morbidity patterns, resource deployment, user attitudes, and changes in health status in Albury-Wodonga.

In August 1975, seven months after it began its work, the Health Study Team submitted its report to the Health Planning Team and formally disbanded.

Case Study 2

The second example of health services planning centres around the new town of Milton Keynes, England. This example exposes some of the conditions within which planners work: the influence of historical developments, the designation of planning responsibility and local political considerations are particularly relevant here. In Milton Keynes, the nature of many of these conditions had to do with the fact that health services planning was a part-time *ad hoc* undertaking, principalled primarily by physicians and medical administrators. I will concentrate on the circumstances which led to the publication of *A Health Service for Milton Keynes*, in December 1968, and to the establishment of a committee charged with overseeing health services planning in the new town until reorganisation of the British National Health Service (NHS) in 1974.

'Until 1974 there was no formal or explicit planning system in the NHS'. (Levitt, 1976, p. 48.) With reorganisation of the NHS a formal planning cycle was imposed upon all regional, area and district health authorities, but previous to that it was

not the specific duty of any one person or any one branch of the health service to initiate comprehensive health planning. In new communities, initiatives have come [sic] from local health authorities, Regional Hospital Boards and Executive Councils, or on occasion, from a medical school or, in some New Towns, from a Development Corporation. (Draper *et al.*, 1971, p. 10.)

In Milton Keynes an initiative to undertake comprehensive health
services planning eventually resulted in the formation of '*ad hoc*
planning machinery for health services', which ceased to exist with
NHS reorganisation (Milton Keynes Health Services – MKHS, 1974,
p. 1).[7]

Detailed planning was conducted by various working groups and
sub-committees which issued reports at irregular intervals from 1969
to 1974. The framework for continuing planning work was established
in *A Health Service for Milton Keynes* which was accepted by local
health agencies in 1969 and was accompanied by the establishment of
the Health Services Liaison Committee. Subsequently, under the
Liaison Committee

> [working groups] were supplied with copies of 'A Health Service
> for Milton Keynes' and were given free rein to consider best how
> their services could be developed in keeping with the general
> philosophy of the document. (Gooding and Reid, 1970, p. 178.)

The Authority to Plan

The designation of a geographic area as a new town in Britain results in
temporary alterations to the administrative responsibilities of the local
authority. These alterations complicate organisation for the planning
and provision of health services among other infrastructural services
in the community.[8]

Ebenezer Howard's original garden city plans only tangentially
included health facilities provision by referring to a centrally located
hospital. However Abercrombie's (1945) Greater London Plan and the
New Towns Committee (Reith Committee) report (Great Britain, 1946),
both highly instrumental in the enactment of the 1946 New Towns
Act, analysed the impact of health services needs on new communities
in some detail. Abercrombie's plan proposed a joint health services
planning body consisting of local planning and hospital authorities.
His recommendations spelled out general procedures for planning
community health services around London and clearly defined the
necessity for integrated planning of health facilities with the larger
community plan:

> Each joint authority would assess the hospital needs of its area and
> the available hospital resources, and work out a plan of hospital
> arrangements for the area . . . All this would be done in consul-
> tation of local professional opinion and other local interests,

including the voluntary hospitals.

The need for consultation and co-operation between these joint hospital authorities and planning authorities is evident. Each can greatly help the other in certain parts of their respective work. It is far too early to suggest the exact form of co-operation. All that can be said at this time is . . . each community in the Region should at the earliest possible stage, seek to define the provision in its community and neighbourhood plans. Large elements of the hospital system would be fixed by existing buildings; some would have to be added to the community plans. Many smaller elements such as health centres, clinics and child welfare centres would be included in neighbourhood plans. (Abercrombie, 1945, p. 121.)

The Reith Committee report included health services planning as one of ten principal factors affecting the preparation of new town plans. It went on to recommend catchment populations and functional content for general, intermediate and specialist hospitals; health centres; maternity and child welfare clinics; and day nurseries. (Great Britain, 1946.)

The 1946 New Towns Act instituted development corporations as the principal planning agencies for new towns. In each new town, a development corporation was empowered

(a)   to acquire, hold, manage and dispose of land and other property;

(b)   to carry out building and other operations;

(c)   to provide water, electricity, gas, sewerage and other services;

(d)   to carry on any business or undertakings in or for the purposes of the new town,

and generally to do anything necessary or expedient for the purposes of the new town or for purposes incidental thereto. (Great Britain, 1965, p. 2.)

The development corporation was given 'all the powers that an ordinary large-scale developing landowner would possess, plus one or two ancillary powers usually exercised by local authorities' (Osborn and Whittick, 1963, p. 88); however, it did not replace the local authorities in the new town's designated area. The corporation was expected to work in co-ordination with existing local authorities, but not to supersede the existing powers of those authorities. On the contrary, the New Towns Act specified that the corporation had power, if not obligation, to contribute to the finance of essential services in the new town if the town's growth imposed too great a burden upon the local authority's own financial and technical resources. (Great Britain, 1972, p. 7.)

Which services were to be provided by the development corporation and which by local authorities, unless specified in the New Towns Act, was supposedly determined through joint development corporation-local authority consultations. In actuality, because local authorities assess and collect rates and development corporations do not, services normally financed through the rates remained within the statutory and fiscal jurisdiction of the local authorities. These rate-borne services included many relating to personal and environmental health. But local authorities did not have sole responsibility for providing health services.

Prior to reorganisation in 1974, the National Health Service consisted of a tri-partite structure: Regional Hospital Boards and their associated Hospital Management Committee, borough or county Executive Councils, and local authorities.

Regional Hospital Boards were responsible to the Ministry of Health for the efficient functioning and distribution of hospital and specialist services in their respective areas, with Hospital Management Committees taking direct responsibility for the operations of individual hospitals or groups of hospitals. Executive Councils, which corresponded approximately to borough or county jurisdictions, were also immediately responsible to the Ministry of Health. The provision of general medical services, maternity medical services, general dental and ophthalmic services, and pharmaceutical services within its designated area was the task of the Executive Council. Working in co-ordination with the Executive Council was a group of local subcommittees, each responsible for one of the areas of health care provision. The third division of the National Health Service, again directly accountable to the Ministry, was made up of local health authorities. This was usually the health department of the local county council or county borough council. The health department was responsible for health centres, ambulance service, ante-natal care, day nurseries, domiciliary nursing and midwifery, community mental health, vaccination and immunisation services, and other preventive medical care. In addition, the county or borough councils were also responsible, under the National Health Service Act, for environmental health services, such as water supply, sewerage, refuse disposal and control of infectious disease.

Despite arguments put forward in the Greater London Plan and in the Reith report for development corporations and local health authorities to share responsibility in the planning and provision of health services in new towns, no legislative action was taken to ensure such co-operation.[9] As a result, as Draper's (1971) study points out, no one person or branch within the health services or the development corporation had the specific duty to initiate health services planning for new towns.

Some attempts were made to establish informal liaison between development corporations and local health authorities in the early new towns (see Sichel, 1969). But with the absence of any clear designation of authority to undertake health services planning, new town managers often relied on the NHS to take care of health services provision.

> The Town Manager, although anxious to liaise, was often appointed to an area which at that stage was little more than a mud flat or rough grassland. He had as yet no general practitioners in the area and no idea from where they would come eventually. He did not know the various peculiarities of the medical profession and its structure and was often reluctant to become involved in professional differences. He was uncertain of the correct stages of procedure, of whom to consult with first; since the National Health Service existed, the Manager usually decided to let the established agencies deal with the situation. (Fry and McKenzie, 1966, p.11.)

Nevertheless, plans for quickly changing demographic and social patterns in new towns prompted some development corporations to press local health agencies to produce plans for health services which responded to the development corporation's need for comprehensive town planning. However, Regional Hospital Boards and, to some extent, Executive Councils and local health departments were responsible for providing their particular ranges of health services to a population larger than that of the new town. Such plans as these separate agencies did produce were directed towards what were seen as needs of persons already in the area; new towns' future populations were unidentified. As a consequence, although projected growth of new town populations required attention, the health needs of future new town residents had to take their place alongside other, already present regional and local health needs.

The resulting difficulties which arose between the development corporations and the NHS authorities were summarised by Dillane (1966, p. 31), who observed after a study of general practice in nineteen new towns, 'New towns and the National Health Service grew up together but there is little evidence of any mutual advantages having resulted'.

That was the way it was when Milton Keynes was designated as a new town in January 1967.

Organising 'Planning Machinery'

The Northampton, Bedford and North Buckinghamshire study which the Ministry of Housing and Local Government published in October 1965 concluded that a new city for 250,000 people in North Buckinghamshire was feasible. In the light of these conclusions the Minister of Housing and Local Government made a Draft Designation Order for an area of 10,500 hectares (25,000 acres) as a result of which a public inquiry was held in July 1966. Early, in 1967 he decided to designate under the New Towns Act about 9,000 hectares (22,000 acres) including the existing towns of Bletchley, Wolverton, and Stoney Stratford as a site for a new city. He also decided that it should be called Milton Keynes, the name of a small village in the designated area. . .

The Milton Keynes Development Corporation was established in May 1967 and drew up a brief specifying its requirements for the preparation of a Plan for the new city. The Corporation then selected the planning consultants and their co-consultants and work on the preparation of the Plan for the new city began in December 1967. (MKDC, 1970, p. 3.)

At the time of its designation, Milton Keynes new town had a population of approximately 40,000. Apart from the newly established Development Corporation, those authorities which had responsibilities for the provision of health services in Milton Keynes in 1967 were Oxford Regional Hospital Board; Buckinghamshire County Council; Bletchley, Newport Pagnell and Wolverton Urban and Newport Pagnell and Winslow Rural District Councils; and Buckinghamshire Executive Council with its Local Medical Committee. These bodies made up the local tripartite (regional board, local authorities and executive council) structure of the NHS (see Figure 4.2).

Moves toward a liaison between these various bodies began within weeks of designation of the new town. In the absence of a single

Figure 4.2: Milton Keynes Area Plan

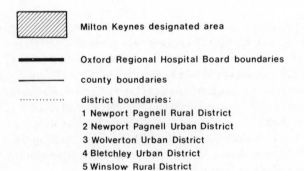

Milton Keynes designated area

Oxford Regional Hospital Board boundaries

county boundaries

district boundaries:
1 Newport Pagnell Rural District
2 Newport Pagnell Urban District
3 Wolverton Urban District
4 Bletchley Urban District
5 Winslow Rural District

Source: Milton Keynes Development Corporation (1970) and Great Britain (1974).

authority 'charged with responsibility for the initiation of health services planning at the local level', the Buckinghamshire Medical Officer of Health and the Senior Administrative Medical Officer of Oxford Regional Hospital Board 'decided to start the process' (Reid and Gooding, 1975, p. 432). At the end of June 1967, formal communication between the Regional Board and the Development Corporation was begun. As a result, the first formal meeting between health and town planning agencies was held on 9 October 1967, attended by the Chairman and the Managing Director of the Development Corporation, a principal of the Corporation's consultant planners, the Chairman of the Regional Board, and the two initiating medical officers.

During the meeting, in addition to designing the composition of a working party which would consult with town planners over health services provision, the participants discussed six factors which were seen to affect health services provision in Milton Keynes: 'people coming to Milton Keynes', 'industry', 'transport in relation to accident potential', 'houses for hospital staff', 'support services for hospital', and the 'link with education, particularly nurses' training'. Consideration of health services focussed on the need for a hospital. A suggestion was put forward that a population of 100,000 would support a new hospital and, based on estimates of population growth, this would occur in approximately ten years.

The Framework for Planners. The working party was quickly assembled and during the following five weeks two meetings were held to 'provide a tentative starting point for consideration by those concerned in the planning of medical and related services for Milton Keynes'. The arguments presented and the decisions taken in these meetings established a framework for the health services plan which eventually was to be produced. Seven points are minuted.

First, it was agreed that health services planning for Milton Keynes should be conducted by a joint committee of all three branches of the NHS, each branch represented by two doctors. The joint committee would work in close liaison with the Development Corporation and their consultant planners; it would seek additional advice from other bodies, such as the Royal College of General Practitioners, as required. This arrangement had already been approved by local general practitioners in deliberation with the Regional Board and the County Health Committee.

Second, the joint committee would report to parent bodies and to the Development Corporation. The Corporation's consultant planners, the managing director of the Corporation and the County Architect and Planning Officer were to be informed of the committee's work.

Third, information was required from the town planners. This included demographic data on projected population, information which was required immediately to determine 'the population of basic planning units'. It was assumed that the age structure of Milton Keynes' population, in keeping with the patterns of other new towns, would be predominantly young; but further information about the population's rate of growth and settlement pattern was needed. Health services planning would consider also the type of industrial development in the new town both as a determinant of occupational health needs and so that the Regional Board could decide whether its industrial activity (catering, laundry, etc.) could be sited separately from medical care facilities. The town planners were expected to supply information on population and industry and also about future patterns of higher education, so that links could be established with professional training programmes; and about future transport systems so that hospitals, health centres and other buildings could be sited.

Fourth, it was deemed desirable to inform the Development Corporation of likely building site requirements as soon as possible, especially for the hospital. Alternative hospital types and sites were discussed at the meetings: a single large general hospital; two district general hospitals; a central acute hospital with various inter-mediate support hospitals which would admit primarily patients for 'social reasons' but also those from the acute hospital who no longer required specialist or intensive care. 'Irrespective of the type of hospital provision', it was agreed that

> there will require to be a peripheral system of health centres as well as the full range of residential facilities for such groups as the elderly and the mentally subnormal.

Health centres were discussed to some detail. It was pointed out that, with an average of 2,000 persons per general practitioner and a 'commonly suggested' maximum size for physician group practices of five or six practitioners, it would be necessary to have two group practices working from a single health centre serving a neighbourhood population of 20,000. However, it was stated that further consideration would have to be given to distances between health centres and served population, particularly with the trend of 'surgery consultation' as distinct from 'domiciliary consultation'.

Fifth, the group considered arrangements for medical staff in Milton Keynes. In line with the desire to 'unify' health services provision, the need to unify health services personnel teams was expressed. It was stated that the general practitioner would continue in the role of 'primary provider' of health services. In addition, planning would look to general practitioners to provide personalised skills in the hospital. This was seen to be of particular help should an intermediate hospital plan be adopted.

Sixth, it was agreed that a unified patient records system would be desirable.

Seventh, ties with medical schools were discussed as means to conduct socio-medical studies, demand analyses and operational research which could help health services planning at Milton Keynes.

The seven points recorded in the minutes of the two meetings put forward a pattern of hospital and health centre provision which was to be maintained throughout subsequent planning. This pattern, although only proposed as a series of alternatives, reflected the prevailing view within the NHS concerning distribution of health services facilities. Health centres had been discussed since the beginning of the NHS as a means to strengthen community health services despite both professional and administrative opposition (see Crossman, 1972 and Hart, 1971b). In 1961, district general hospitals had been designated within main centres of population throughout England and Wales in order to centralise specialty and acute medical services. In fact, these early meetings at Milton Keynes were taking place during a time when district general hospitals were being re-defined by the Bonham-Carter Committee as centres accommodating a full range of acute and chronic illness services, each serving a population of at least 200,000. (Great Britain, 1969.)

The planning framework which emerged from the two meetings also specified the composition of the health services planning team. Each branch of the NHS was to be represented on the committee by two physicians. Although liaison with town planners and other local officials was agreed in the name of comprehensive provision, it appears that proposals on health services which were to be put forward to the Development Corporation and to the local health authorities were intended to be drafted within a strictly medical group.

Constituting and Empowering the Medical Planning Group. Before the new joint committee was appointed, an argument arose between the health authorities over which was empowered to do what in Milton Keynes.

In early December 1967, the Town Manager of Bletchley sent a letter to the Managing Director of the Development Corporation, stating, in part, 'My council has decided that the time has gone for the Hospital Authorities to be allowed to "dither" further and they [the council] are asking the Member of Parliament to arrange for a deputation to meet the Minister of Health.'

Several years earlier, a seventeen and one-half acre hospital site in Bletchley, adjacent to an existing maternity and out-patient unit, had been agreed upon by the Bletchley Urban District Council, the Regional Hospital Board and county planning and educational officers. The District Council had reserved the site for acute hospital development. Now the Town Manager was requesting the Development Corporation's support to consider this site within the new town master plan at 'an urgent date'.

Such independent action on the part of the District Council, which would threaten the tightly defined and 'unified' framework drafted by local health officials during the previous two months, is not surprising given the notable exclusion of district officials from the organising meetings. Local community representatives who had participated in providing the tentative 'starting point' for health services planning had been general practitioners approved by the Local Medical Council. No non-medical community representatives had been present.

The Corporation's Managing Director informed the Bletchley Town Manager that the Development Corporation Board would consider the District Council's request at its January meeting. At the same time, the Managing Director passed on a copy of the Bletchley letter to the working party chairman, commenting that the Corporation would not support any hospital development in Bletchley 'until the whole matter of medical services has been considered by all concerned'. The working party chairman replied that 'it would be quite premature to consider one particular detail of the medical service for Milton Keynes prior to agreement on their likely overall pattern'. The Bletchley Council letter was also passed on to the Regional Hospital Board with a request for advice.

Following this latter correspondence, Oxford Regional Hospital Board issued a press release, on 13 December, addressing 'Hospital Services in the North Buckinghamshire Area'. The substance of the press release, in addition to listing the existing hospital provision in the area, was a statement of Regional Hospital Board policy that 'until such time as Milton Keynes itself justifies its own specific hospital services' need for such services in North Buckinghamshire would be met by existing facilities or already planned major hospitals in adjacent towns (i.e., Aylesbury and Northampton). The Regional Hospital Board stated that it was aware of the inconvenience to some rural areas which would result from this policy and, therefore, it had provided diagnostic clinics in Bletchley and Wolverton. The press release further stated that since the designation of Milton Keynes as a new town the Regional Hospital Board had been considering the need for a hospital there and it was now involved in discussion of a comprehensive range of services. However, the Board's statement emphasised that during the early years of development, especially with uncertainties over population growth, no commitment could be taken to provide hospital services.[10]

After continued consultation with working party members, the Development Corporation Board decided at its January meeting that the Bletchley proposal

> impinged upon the development responsibilities of the Corporation and, although it was not a new proposal, the [Corporation] Board was in complete agreement with the view expressed by the Oxford Regional Hospital Board that hospital development as proposed by the [Bletchley District] Council must await preparation and development of the overall plan for health services.

This decision effectively ended the moves of any local authority acting independently of the envisaged joint committee in health services provision. Without Development Corporation support any such action was doomed to failure.

While these exchanges were being made, the joint committee was being constituted and was conducting discussion and seminars on health services provision in Milton Keynes. The committee was called the Medical Planning Group. All five members of the initial working party which had established the framework for health services planning were members. Three additional Buckinghamshire County Council medical officers, two more local general practitioners, a chief medical officer from the field of occupational health, and two observers from the Ministry of Health also took part in the work of the Group. The county Medical Officer served as the Planning Group's chairman.

The first of several seminars was held in December 1967.

The presentations at the seminars were widely based. For example, in looking at health service planning there was no reference to whether there should be a hospital or to where health centres might be sited in Milton Keynes. Instead, the discussions were centred on such philosophical questions as the likely future relationship between the prevention and cure of disease, or between the hospital and community aspects of care. (de Monchaux *et al.*, 1969, p.4.)

By the following March, a document had been produced by the Medical Planning Group which described 'The Early Stage of Health Service Planning' for Milton Keynes. In the report — which was not published — some discussion was given to 'philosophical questions' but more was devoted to specific service provision.

About hospitals, one member wrote:

The Oxford Regional Hospital Board is enthusiastically co-operating with the local health authority and the general practitioners in attempting to plan a fully integrated health service for the development area. The concept of a district general hospital is already felt to be somewhat out of date, and while developments at Northampton and Aylesbury are proceeding on these lines and will help to carry the interim load of the new city, it may be that parts of the traditional hospital service will not be identified at Milton Keynes. It is hoped to adopt a new approach to the hospital needs of a community and there are several considerations which will affect planning in the early stages. (Medical Planning Group — MPG, 1968a, p. 4.)

By June the Medical Planning Group 'had agreed to look at health services as a whole irrespective of any present legal or financial obstacles'. In an 'update' of the March report made to the Development Corporation, the Medical Planning Group reported that it had firmly accepted the idea of a single hospital in Milton Keynes. 'All remaining aspects of medical practice would be provided at health centres.' Subsequently provision for a district general hospital on a 'single campus' was incorporated in the consultants' plans.

'A Health Service for Milton Keynes'

Several meetings were held between the Medical Planning Group and various health and town planning officials between June and December 1968. Discussions at the Group meetings essentially composed the health services planning process. The work of the Planning Group consisted almost entirely of 'planning by [the] consensus' which emerged from discussions (Gooding and Reid, 1970). No epidemiological or demographic studies are evidenced in the Planning Group's minutes. At the end of the year the Medical Planning Group submitted its report (MPG, 1968b). There were no substantive differences between the proposals put forward in *A Health Service for Milton Keynes* and the 'tentative starting points' established by the *ad hoc* working party in October and November 1967.

The report proposed that most 'peripheral services' — regarded as prevention and primary care, including general practitioner services — be based in health centres, each serving a population of approximately 30,000. Minor diagnostic and therapeutic work was to take place in the health centre. Domiciliary care would be provided by community health teams working from the health centres. Hostel and day care facilities were suggested to accommodate other peripheral services, such as care of the elderly and the mentally ill, which could not be supplied entirely from the health centres. Other proposals included a full-time occupational health specialist working with local general practitioners; an assessment centre for handicapped children; links between health centres and educational facilities; and programmes of environmental and health education.

'The major central services', as distinct from 'peripheral services', were to be 'based in the hospital which provides the various specialist medical facilities for the surrounding population' (p. 15). The hospital was to include specialist diagnostic services, in-patient care, rehabilitation services, an accident and emergency unit, and maternity and psychiatric services. Some out-patient and day services were also envisaged in the hospital. The Oxford Regional Record Linkage Scheme would extend to include Milton Keynes. In addition, the report proposed a postgraduate centre associated with the hospital and the secondment of medical undergraduates to Milton Keynes, at first to health centres and eventually to the hospital as well. This secondment programme, the report stated, 'would be greatly facilitated by the provision of suitable living accommodation in relation to the hospital site' (p. 24) — an 'interest' voiced at the first formal meeting.

The report specified that 'there should be a single central hospital campus on which would be situated the central acute unit with other types of units grouped around it' (p. 27). The hospital complex would

serve 'the total needs' of Milton Keynes, and, consequently, subsequent 'detailed planning' would have to create 'appropriate
environments for the various activities of the hospital' to accommodate
possible expansion and 'urgent and unpredictable demands'.

Other aspects of health services provision were discussed in the
forty-page report: ambulance services, social work, research, and
staffing among them. No time schedule was proposed for the actual
provision of services although the report suggested the first health
centre would be required in the early 1970s.

Formalising the Planning Machinery. On 22 January 1969 the Medical
Planning Group met to consider its next step. The Group's report had
been approved by the local Executive Council, the County Health
Committee, the Development Corporation, and the Executive
Committee of Oxford Regional Health Board. The Planning Group now
saw a 'need to formalize machinery for future detailed planning'. The
proposed structure which emerged from this meeting was subsequently
approved by the three NHS agencies.[11]

A Health Services Liaison Committee was established to advise constituent bodies on the co-ordination of all health services in Milton
Keynes and to undertake suggested tasks for constituent bodies. The
Chairman of the Development Corporation, was invited to chair the
Liaison Committee. The Committee membership was composed of
three representatives each from the Regional Hospital Board, the
local Executive Council, the County Medical Committee, and the
Development Corporation. Observers were invited from the newly
formed Department of Health and Social Security and from the
consultant planners. Several members of the Medical Planning Group
were to continue as members of the Liaison Committee.

> The matters to be placed before the Joint Liaison Committee would
> be coordinated [sic] by a Joint Working Party consisting of all
> officer members of the liaison committee and including represent-
> atives of the following health services professions:— Doctors,
> dentists, nurses, pharmacists, opticians, registered medical auxiliaries
> and health service social workers. (MKHS, 1969.)

Once again, the county Medical Officer was named chairman of the
Joint Working Party.

The Joint Working Party, which replaced the Medical Planning
Group as the 'central feature' of the health services planning structure,

was to be assisted by 'parallel working parties dealing with the development of buildings and with administration and finance respectively' (Gooding and Reid, 1970, p. 177). In addition, the Joint Working Party was to establish 'a series of working groups, some concerned with particular professions [e.g., nursing, dental] and others with services [e.g. child health, care of the elderly] ', and these were 'given a free hand in preparing suggested schemes for providing the best possible health service for the future citizens of Milton Keynes', so long as they kept within the 'general philosophy' of *A Health Service for Milton Keynes* (pp. 177–8).

This structure continued to operate as the health services planning agencies of Milton Keynes until April 1974 when NHS reorganisation made it redundant.

Continued Planning. By June 1969, discussion on the site and construction of the district general hospital had begun between the Chief Architect and the Regional Hospital Board and representatives of the Development Corporation. The first phase was expected to be required in operation during the period 1976 to 1978.

In September 1969, the Liaison Committee considered the possibility of adopting a community hospital plan which would entail the staffing of in-patient services by general practitioners. This concept arose from mention of 'small hospitals in peripheral towns' in the recently published Bonham-Carter report. In November 1969, discussions were held with local general practitioners regarding 'Apportionment of Functions between Hospital and Health Centre', a Joint Working Party working paper which emphasised the specialist nature of the proposed hospital. Most discussion focused on the need for health centres.

At the December 1969 meeting of the Liaison Committee, during discussion of alternative hospital sites, the idea of a community hospital was resurrected. In response, a consultant to the Development Corporation emphasised the need for a fixed hospital site and following the meeting the presently designated site for a district general hospital was agreed. The idea of a community hospital in Milton Keynes was not discarded, however. Toward the end of 1969, the Joint Working Party considered a paper which was submitted by the Oxford Regional Hospital Board and which discussed the organisation of district general and community hospitals in the Oxford Region. The Regional Hospital Board proposed over twenty possible 'peripheral Community Hospitals' in the Region, one of which was at Milton Keynes 'as the first stage of the district general hospital' (MKHS, 1969, p. 18). The paper invited opinions on the proposals, especially on the 'type and range of medical cases which can be appropriately nursed in the Community Hospital', among other points. This two-phase development of what would eventually be a district general hospital was accepted by the Joint Working Party. The Community Hospital was envisaged to open during 1976.

In 1970, however, the Government's Green Paper on the future structure of the NHS began to dominate many considerations for future health services provision. As a result, work on the planning of a hospital for Milton Keynes was in effect suspended. In its final report the Joint Working Party summarised the progress on hospital development by explaining that 'due to uncertainties about capital finance from the Department of Health and Social Security' the Working Party was presented with an 'inability to programme development of a district general hospital'. However, 'Milton Keynes district general hospital should be programmed to start building in 1976/77' (MKHS, 1974, p. 173).

Work on other areas did continue, however. Working parties produced papers throughout the four year period outlining, for the most part, operational policies and staffing requirements, and the service relationship between various elements in the health system.

The most visible product of the planning effort was the provision of health centres. By the end of 1971, the requirement for five permanent and four temporary health centres had been established by the Joint Working Party. Within two years one of the permanent sites had been opened and another was under construction. When the Joint Working Party ceased its existence in 1974, the other permanent health centre was about to be completed and three more were under construction, including one which was located on part of the site designated for the hospital.

With reorganisation of the NHS all *ad hoc* 'machinery' for health services planning ceased. A Development Corporation/Health Services Liaison Committee was established 'to identify areas in which there appeared to be a need for further coordination between the Development Corporation and Health Services Authorities'. Statutory responsibility for planning health services for Milton Keynes passed to Aylesbury District, Buckinghamshire Area and Oxford Regional Health Authorities.

Some Observations

Health Services for a New City and *A Health Service for Milton Keynes* are not typical of health services planning work. Both projects dealt with new towns entailing rapidly growing populations and few existing services. Both were conducted by specially constituted planning teams. Typically, health services planning is the charge of an established or permanent agency whose action space includes not only the allocation of future resources and services but also the continuing management of a slowly evolving and considerably larger stock of existing resources.

But the very things which make the Albury-Wodonga and the Milton Keynes health services plans atypical also allow for a more easily comprehensible and perhaps more incisive view of health services planning work and its course towards the production of a health services plan. The *ad hoc* nature of the new town health services plans provides a beginning and an end of a study of large-scale resource allocation and hence encapsulates the nature of health services planning.

Although it is not appropriate to generalise from the two examples, they do demonstrate several things about health services planning work. It is clear that health services planning can be, and is, conducted in a process-oriented manner. Health services planning can, indeed, be regarded as another branch of what Robinson called 'a family of disciplines and activities which plan and use planning techniques'. As in town planning, goals may be set, alternatives may be evaluated, and preferred plans may be selected in health services planning. Health services planning is also an activity fraught with problems which may seem to the planner to do little more than detract from his or her work. Local disputes about who plans and the powerful influence of prevailing medical views are only two examples.

But what is of particular interest in comparing the two planning projects is the dissimilarity of their respective processes despite the commonality of their products. In terms of resource deployment, the health services plans proposed in *Health Services for a New City* and *A Health Service for Milton Keynes* are not dissimilar. Both plans suggest development of a system of decentralised health centres and continuing care services and the development of centralised acute services. The plan for Albury-Wodonga is somewhat more detailed in specifying functional contents of health service facilities, timing of development and organisation of ongoing planning, among other things. But, for the most part, the end products of planning have a lot in common. Yet the planning process in each was different. The Albury-Wodonga work entailed a highly structured, step-by-step methodology; the Milton Keynes work was undertaken primarily in the form of team discussions.

It is difficult to attribute results to particular aspects or phases of work. It seems to me, however, that the difference between the two planning approaches outlined in the examples above may be explained by the difference in who the planners were in each case.

In the case of Milton Keynes, the planning team members, first in the Medical Planning Group and later in the Joint Working Party, brought to the planning work knowledge and expertise which seems to have enabled them to share a common view of the health services needs of the new town. All of the planners were physicians, whose medical skills and experiences may well have contributed to a general agreement, from the beginning of their work, about what health services were required and about what facilities those services entailed.

Clearly, the common knowledge played no small role in the resolution of problems relating to whose responsibility it was to establish priorities for health services in Milton Keynes. In the absence of any formalised or statutory authority for doing so, concerned physicians came together to plan health services, to the almost complete exclusion of non-medical participants.

The 'unique opportunity to plan health services [at Milton Keynes] uninhibited by constraints' (Reid and Gooding, 1975, p. 436) was seized by the Medical Planning Group to essentially restate and impose prevailing ideas on health services provision. The concept of health centre-based primary care services operating around a centralised district general hospital, for example, was widely held and promoted within the NHS at the time. Planning did not occur as a disciplined process. Goals were not formally set, demographic studies were not undertaken, alternative patterns of delivery were not fully developed nor investigated. Despite formalised planning procedures, however, the plan which was proposed reflected a knowledgeable sensitivity to what the planning team recognised as the needs of the new town. The jurisdiction of medical knowledge extended to set the pattern for planning health services delivery in a rather discursive fashion.

On the other hand, the Albury-Wodonga work was highly procedural. Goals were set, alternatives were developed and assessed, and from an evaluation of alternative delivery strategies a preferred strategy was selected. At the same time, the work was overtly not medically-oriented.

The keystone to the Albury-Wodonga planning work was the Study Team's attempt to separate areas of medical jurisdiction from planning jurisdiction. This is seen in the Team's identification of medical strategy as 'a body of knowledge and capabilities' and the distinction of medical strategy from the planning of delivery strategies which 'ensure that the entire body of the same medical knowledge and capabilities is available within the community health programme'. In effect, a line was drawn, after the completion of the Medical Strategy Matrix, demarcating in the planning work the end of required medical expertise and the beginning of predominantly planning expertise. Once community health tasks were identified and arrayed in the Medical Strategy Matrix, they served as building blocks with which planners designed physical groups of health services which had already been agreed as medically correct. Later attempts were made to bridge medical strategy and delivery strategy with the evaluative use of goals which had been previously agreed but which were too broadly defined to provide strong direction for the construction of alternative patterns of health services. In the end, the distinction between medical strategy and delivery strategy seems to have implicitly assumed the non-contestability of medical strategy. Health tasks of medical strategy were objectified and, once agreed upon, were stated as given.

Now, the Albury-Wodonga Health Study Team was led by non-medicos, by planning consultants whose expertise rested on management and physical design skills. There could be no assumed common medical knowledge between the non-medico and medico members of the Study Team, nor between the Study Team as a whole and its supervisory Health Planning Team. If only to establish, in the eyes of participating medicos, their own credibility and capability as health services planners, the consultant planners may have sought to identify a body of work over which they could exercise some recognised professional authority. Ergo, the definition of delivery strategy as an essentially non-medical entity.

This is, to be sure, largely conjecture. But it is not unreasonable conjecture. Planners influence planning, by who they are and by how they think. That the plans they produce may seem to be little affected by that influence is the focus of the rest of this book.

Notes

1.   Health services are not nationalised in Australia nor, during the time of the health services planning project, was health insurance. Although the

152   *Case Studies*

organisation of health service authorities differs between the several states of
Australia, each of the states is individually 'responsible for providing the public
health systems and mental health facilities and for maintaining the public
hospitals' for its own residents (Sax, 1972, p. 123). Primary medical services are
privately provided as are some additional hospital services.

2.   The account of this plan relies heavily on the Study Team's report,
Health Services for a New City: A Guide for Action (Albury-Wodonga Development Corporation, 1976) of which I was an author. I worked as one of the full-
time health services planners on the Albury-Wodonga Health Study Team while
in the employ of a private consulting firm and as field work for my doctoral thesis.

Other members of the Study Team were Mr E. John Cooper (Project
Director) of Llewelyn-Davies Kinhill; Dr Jerry Krupinski, Director of Research at
the Victoria Mental Health Authority; and Dr David Jones of the New South
Wales Health Commission. Professor E. Maurice Backett, Head of the Department
of Community Health, University of Nottingham, and Dr Cyril J. Cummins,
formerly of the New South Wales Department of Health, served as consultants.
The Health Planning Team was chaired by Mr D. Winterbottom, Chief Planner
of the Albury-Wodonga Development Corporation, to whom I am grateful for
permission to have used this study in my research and to quote extensively
from the planning report here.

3.   See Chapter 1.

4.   Following formal completion of the strategic health services planning
work, one of the participant health agencies would comment critically upon the
Study Team's approach: 'it is simply a method of organising information,
about which subjective decisions have been made, into an orderly and logical
sequence'. (Personal correspondence.)

5.   Several days before the Health Study Team submitted its draft report
to the Health Planning Team in August 1975, the Albury-Wodonga Development
Corporation adopted a southern option for growth, entailing first expansion in
the Wodonga area. The sensitivity of various delivery strategies to the two
growth options fomed an important part of the evaluation process in the draft
report. However, in the final report, which was published in January 1976, the
southern direction of growth was assumed and, consequently, was not discussed in
the sensitivity analysis.

6.   During the planning period, the Study Team had been requested by the
Development Corporation to engage in liaison with a local Health Advisory
Committee, one of a series of public Advisory Committees constituted by the
Development Corporation. Community advice was required to evaluate the
alternative delivery strategies against the 'local acceptance' criteria. However,
during meetings with the Health Advisory Committee it became the view of
the Study Team that the local opinion being expressed through this formal body
was being dominated by its medical professional membership, which accounted
for over three-quarters of the Committee. As a result, the Study Team had
approach other non-medical groups within Albury-Wodonga to discuss directions
for health services delivery, an action,which, when compounded by the knowledge
that the full-time health services planners on the Health Study Team were not
medicos, prompted objections from the Health Advisory Committee's chairman.
From this experience the Study Team recommended the separation of health
professional and lay community input, arguing:

Public participation in decision-making is an important element in the
approach to the creation of a new city which has been adopted by the
Development Corporation. Participation by the users of services is also an
integral element in the continuing planning of health services. The users of

health services fall into two distinct groups. First, there is the community at large whose needs services are intended to meet. Second, however, the professional providers of health care are in an important sense users of services. Many of the tasks which are performed within the system take place as part of a direct relationship between an individual health professional and an individual patient. The system as a whole serves an infrastructure which the professional makes use of in the course of his direct relationship with the patient. Continuing planning therefore should provide for participation both by interests within the community at large and by professional health workers who would not necessarily be party to the decision-making councils of the health authorities in the absence of special provision for their participation . . .

It is important that decision-making authorities should know whether views emanating from consultative bodies are representative of the community at large or of providers. (pp. 146, 149.)

7.   Unless otherwise referenced, information relating to the workings of various health services planning groups in Milton Keynes is abstracted from memoranda and correspondence made available for this study by the Aylesbury District Health Authority and by the Milton Keynes Development Corporation. I am grateful to C.H. Wooler, formerly of Aylesbury District Health Authority, and to Peter Waugh, of the Milton Keynes Development Corporation, for their kind assistance.

8.   The history of parliamentary action which instituted new town programmes in Britain is well documented, particularly in the works of Rodwin (1956) and Osborn and Whittick (1963). Similarly, Eckstein (1959), Lindsey (1962) and Forsyth (1973) have written detailed accounts of the conditions which preceded and influenced introduction of the National Health Service.

9.   Neither local government reorganisation in 1972 nor NHS reorganisation in 1974 offset the lack of integration between local health authorities and the NHS. In 1946, during negotiations with the British Medical Association, Minister of Health Aneurin Bevan was forced to compromise on several issues pertaining to the NHS organisation in order to ensure the medical profession's co-operation within the nationalised health service. Among these compromises, responsibility for health services provision was removed from the jurisdiction of local authorities. In 1972, Richard Crossman, an advocate of local authority control of health services during the NHS reorganisation debate, noted that, once again, due mainly to the medical profession's 'veto' such local control 'is not going to happen'. Citing the profession's 'uninformed prejudice . . . that to work under a local authority would be the end of clinical freedom and the end of the doctors' standing in society', Crossman complained:

We are being forced in our planning into a miserable middle way. The new service will neither be taking over those local government areas which are essentially community services, nor will it be taken into local government. It will still be wobbling in between.

. . . A 'managerial philosophy' lies behind the creation of a new 'managerially efficient' health service structure, which shall be filled with men of managerial experience . . . who will have the same self-perpetuating oligarchic attitude or satrapian attitude, which I found when I visited the Regional Hospital Boards — people who are still settled into their entrenched vested interests and could look forward to staying there as long as they like, and spending very large sums of money in a very high-handed way and not having to worry about vague, ill-informed complaints from down below. (1972, pp. 24–6.)

Crossman observed that 'all self-perpetuating oligarchies . . . are aloof and remote from public opinion'. His support of local authority control of health services provision stemmed from the view that 'whatever you may hate in local authorities, there is a certain crude relationship with humanity which one experiences as a result of electoral defeat' (p. 24).

10. Contradicting this statement were the working party's seven 'starting points' which not only included specification of hospital services in Milton Keynes but had also included the desire to inform the Development Corporation of a likely building site for the hospital as soon as possible.

The implication is that it was not the hospital nor the site which was being disputed with Bletchley District Council. Perhaps the area of contention was the authority for specifying health services provision in the new town.

11. Approval of local health authorities seems to have been confined to the county Health Committee and the local Medical Council. There is no record of District participation.

Part Three

'ONLY CONNECT . . .'
(E.M. Forster)

5 SOME POLITICAL THINKING ON PLANNING ACTION

The focus of the third part of this book is on the day-to-day work of health services planners. I will look first at the functions of that work within the context of a capitalist society and then concentrate on how the three dimensions of planning action are influenced by social organisation.

Based on the arguments presented in Part One, I argue that, in a capitalist society, health services planning is one of many state activities which are directed towards the achievement of the state's administrative and legitimatory aims. Although health services are indeed provided partially as a result of health services planning, and working class people do benefit from their provision, the nature and scope of planning action are predominantly defined by the interests and needs of capital. Planners, then, are the technicians who perform the task of allocating politically-prescribed health services, and thereby work to legitimate, and administer to, the needs of capital.

Health services planners are agents of capital, translating capital needs into health care resources and arguing about alternative distributional configurations of health care resources. But the people with whom planners argue are physicians. It is physicians whom the capital-owning class employ to define appropriate units of health care resources, physicians whose class associations to capital and whose own professional power puts them in a much stronger socio-political position than planners. This fight between planners and physicians is essentially one over who controls health services planning and it emerges as part of the prevailing user-provider 'conflict' in health. I argue that this is really a false conflict among agents of capital (some more powerful than others) rather than a conflict between social classes.

Health Services Planning as a State Activity

Health services planning, in most capitalist societies, is primarily a state activity. Like the planning activities directed towards the provision of other nominally public or publicly-regulated services, health services planning has a dual function within the capitalist state. It is both an administrative and a legitimatory activity.

157

Implementation of the product of health services planning, a health services plan, can be used not only to effect some measurable regulation upon the economic cycle, but also to improve the conditions under which capital is accumulated. These results contribute to the fulfillment of the state's administrative function.

Regulation upon the economic cycle is clearly demonstrated in the current decreases in health services expenditure in many capitalist societies. In the face of financial deficits and rapidly increasing costs, state health care budgets are being frozen and, in some cases, actually reduced. Health services planners plan the physical and distributional consequences of such expenditure adjustments, because the state's attempts to help regulate the economy through health services budgeting often has to be translated in the end into new or reduced resource allocations. And this is the job of the planner: to administer the allocation of budgeted resources.

However, the state's administrative role is to balance its regulatory activity with the need to improve or maintain the material substructure which is required for continued capital accumulation. If budgetary constraint in health services provision directly results in untreated illness and in increases in workers' 'days lost', the productivity of a given amount of labour power declines and, consequently, the rate of profit falls. Among other things, labour must be kept healthy enough to work and health services must be provided in order to meet that aim. Again, health services planning is used to administer the provision of those health services, to determine how many health care resources — beds, places, visits, manpower, etc. — have to be provided and where they should go. The uses of cost-benefit and input-output analyses based on 'days of work lost by illness' exemplify the important contribution which health services planning can make to maintaining the conditions required for capital accumulation.

But health services planning, like other forms of state-financed planning, is not promulgated as a means by which owners of capital, through the state, improve conditions for the continued exploitation and accumulation of capital. Health services planning is represented instead as a means by which 'better health services' and 'better health' can be enjoyed by all. It is promoted as the *state's* doing something about health services. And this propagandised view of health services planning, of course, has many benefits for the capital-owning class.

By establishing health services planning as a formal mechanism through which health services are to be provided, the state legitimises its control over the provision of health services and, by doing so, helps to maintain its political capability to administer for the continued accumulation of capital. This is in keeping with the state's legitimatory role to justify its own position. Further, by investing resources in health services planning, the state demonstrates a 'public-minded' concern with which it can assuage social discontent over types and distributions of health services. The state can 'justifiably' argue, 'we are doing something about it,' aided by the formalised aims of health services planning — 'accessibility', 'continuity of care', etc. — which are often so vaguely drafted that they are too good to be critically questioned.

The benefit of promoting health services planning in this way is to delay, if not to suppress, social conflicts. By institutionalising the planning process within the 'legitimate' organisation of the state, the capital-owning class gains some controls over the avenues by which social conflicts present themselves. Conflict, too, becomes largely institutionalised. Protests about 'poor health services', for example, must be taken up with the 'proper authorities' if they are to be politically and publicly acceptable. And these 'proper authorities' are often not authorative at all, but rather take the form of volunteer community groups — such as the health systems agencies in the US or the community health councils in the UK — whose power to deal with protests which are concerned with large-scale change is negligible and often suspect by the community itself. Yet conflicts which present themselves outside of these institutionalised mechanisms are easily derided as inappropriate and illegitimate.

Not only is the presentation of conflict largely restricted to the state's institutionalised activity, but also the manner of conflict is dictated by the manner of the activity. The vocabulary of protest over health services must be the vocabulary in which health services planning activity is undertaken. The use of technical and clinical terminology in considerations of health services planning, even when bowdlerised for layman's consumption, serves to restrict the arena of recognised and acceptable conflict over health services provision primarily to those who can, by education or by freedom of occupation, speak in that vocabulary. This applies primarily to physicians, but also to health administrators and to those with the time to learn the vocabulary themselves.

But as repressive as the commonly-criticised jargon of health and health services planning is the scope of acceptable discussion. Protest about factors which are not recognised as acceptable indices in the state health services planning activity — for example, the alienation of work as a cause of morbidity — goes ignored by state planning agencies. Such protests are left to be voiced outside the state mechanism, where they become immediately 'improper' and 'unacceptable' to the prevailing social ideology. Insofar as the state serves as an arena for political conflict, then, the rules by which that conflict is played out are governed largely by the dominant power within the state.

These legitimatory aims are inseparable from the state's administrative aims. In order to diffuse immediate conflicts emerging from 'class struggle', the dominant capital-owning class will require the provision of more social services, 'especially in the field of collective consumption' (Castells, 1976). This may necessitate, among other things, an expansion in the state-financed health sector, an expansion which serves to diffuse conflict but which simultaneously increases consumption of privately-produced goods (such as 'drugs and bandages') and creates jobs which help to absorb labour surplus, thus indirectly increasing the productivity of a given amount of labour-power. Of course, the working class does benefit materially from improved and expanded health services. But, as Cockburn (1977, p. 55) states,[1] 'As the working class has an interest in receiving services, so capital has an interest in seeing them serviced'. Keeping the working class healthy to work lowers the reproductive costs of labour. At the same time, increasing collective consumption supports the legitimatory functions of the state.

Once again, to legitimate and administer the provision of health services the state employs health services planners:

> State intervention to maintain or extend the market for health goods or services . . . imposes, in the short run, the necessity for some regulation — either through its own bureaucracy or through a delegation of state authority — the most important of which being the 'planning' of the allocation of resources . . . [The] state has to find means to facilitate the geographical and financial access to physicians and to hospitals, and to limit the expensive competition . . . but always with the objective of both satisfying the demand for care and maintaining the overall costs as low as possible. (Renaud, 1975, p. 566.)

Now, the administrative and legitimatory benefits which accrue to the capital-owning class are not unique to the state's health services planning activity. They are present also in the functions fulfilled by other state-financed services, such as those associated with the provision of housing and education. Together, these activities contribute to legitimising the role of the state as administrator of 'public' services and as executive of the economically and politically powerful. More importantly, however, inter-class conflicts are diffused, deflected or made latent. Thus, health services planning, like other forms of state planning, serves as a tool by which the capital-owning class exercises what Lukes calls the third dimension of power. The work of health services planners must be tailored to meet these needs. Planning action must be channelled to achieve the functions of a capitalist state activity.

On the Influence of Social Organisation on Planning Action

The social structures of capitalist society influence health services planning action in all of its dimensions: *what* the planner plans, *what* the planner *does* to plan and *how* the planner plans. These influences may take both a direct form (for example, through the legislative mechanisms of the state) and an indirect form (for example, under the guise of 'inter-professional conflicts').

What the Planner Plans

Chapter 1 discussed how the action space of planning work, *what* the planner plans, is attributable primarily to the administrative and legitimatory activities of the state. Within the state mechanism, the capital-owning class defines the action space of health services planning in such a way that the planning work contributes towards maintaining the economic and ideological conditions required for production and capital accumulation. The state serves as a mechanism by which the capital-owning class prescribes the issues and resources with which health services planning work is to be concerned. The state, embodying the formalised political organisation of the dominant social class, prescribes the issues and problems of the health services planning work-place in order to legitimise its role as well as existing capital accumulation processes and to avoid and suppress possible conflicts which might undermine it. But the nature of the health services to be planned are also defined to service the working class. Thus, health services are important elements in the administration of capitalist society. Health services contribute directly towards meeting the accumulative requirements of the social structure by helping to maintain a 'healthy' labour force — that is, a labour force which is healthy enough to work.

Kelman (1975, p. 634) calls this the 'functional' definition of health wherein ' "health" is subordinated to production rather than an end in itself':

> Functional 'health' is that organismic condition of the population most consistent with, or least disruptive of, the process of capital accumulation. At the individual level this means the capacity to effectively do productive (contributing to accumulation) work. In the aggregate a population is said to be functionally healthy if the expenditures necessary to bring that condition about are not so high as to interfere with the expansion of capital. More precisely, a population is said to be optimally functionally healthy if the last increment of resources directed toward health contributes as much to overall productivity and accumulation as it would if diverted toward direct capital investment (accumulation).

The functional definition of health — or, rather the functional *ideology* of health — determines the types of health services which are required to keep the labour force physically and mentally capable of work. Where priorities in the provision of health services require financial trade-offs, reproduction costs of labour are crucial elements in decision-making.

This is demonstrated in the paradox of increased use of technology and large demands for low-technology, continuing care. A person with a chronic ailment is often either not 'sick enough' to not work or so 'sick' for so long that he or she is not likely to work again. Unskilled workers are more likely to suffer chronic disease than skilled or 'white-collar' workers. On the other hand, members of the labour force with 'high socio-economic status' — i.e., occupation, education and income — and, therefore, whose reproduction costs are high, historically are at least as likely to suffer a heart attack as workers with low socio-economic status.[2] Is there any wonder that there is an emphasis on 'high technology medicine' coincident with a growing incidence (or recognition) of chronic disease and 'low-level' disability?

The range and priorities of health services which are required to meet these incidences of physiological 'dysfunction' are the objects whose provision the health services planner is given to plan. These prescribed 'functional' services must be moderated by the further administrative need to minimise social expenses and maximise profit, and by the legitimatory need to balance between ideal conditions for capital accumulation and the assuagement of social discontent. Leaving 'unproductive' elderly to die off, for example, though economically profitable for capital, would prove socially costly to its interests.

Capitalist society requires a 'work-able' working class. Health 'dysfunction' must be diagnosed and technically repaired. For the administrative purposes of capital, health needs are the resources which most 'effectively and efficiently' restore unhealthy people to an acceptable level of productive capacity. For the planner, this results in an operational leap from individual health needs to health care resources, a leap which ignores consideration of the services which those needs may require.

Here the role of the physican is important. Later in this chapter I will discuss the apparent conflict between physicians and planners over health care resources, but it is important now to emphasise one point in relation to definitions and prescriptions of the health services for which planners plan. Physicians comply with the needs of capital by prescribing health care requirements in ways which protect their professional power within the prevailing structure of society. In order to maintain what Johnson refers to as a profession's social distance, and thereby to control its work, the medical profession expresses individual health needs as requirement for hospital beds, physiotherapy sessions, day care programmes, and the physician's own time, among other resource packages. Individuals in need of services depend upon the physician to prescribe the resources required to treat their health needs. By exercising its occupational control, by reducing the common area of professional-client knowledge, by prescribing health services requirement in terms of resource require-ments, physicians too serve as agents of capital. Resource requirements can be easily managed in terms of functional output per unit of financial input and to avoid the problems associated with definitions of health.[3]

These prescribed resources become the composite elements – the 'object-resources' – of the planner's action space. Little latitude is allowed for alternative resource configurations, especially those which may challenge the power of capital or the powerful professional interests serving capital. Little scope is available for experimenting with different ways of providing services which are required to meet individual needs.

For the health services planner, none of these legitimatory and administrative machinations may be apparent. Instead, new government policies supporting 'expansion of residential services', for example, are directed through the state hierarchy to the health services planner's workplace. 'Expansion of residential services' is the order of the day

and the planner's job is to carry out the planning steps which that
order requires.

Operational Activities and the Health Services Planner's Role

The operational activities of planning and the planner's role are in-
trinsically related in health services planning work. In turn, they are
influenced significantly by the composition of action space. My
interest in exploring this relationship is not with what techniques are
employed in the several phases of health services planning work, but
with the ideological role which underlies what the health services
planner does.

'Neutralist', 'advocate' or 'activist' health services planners cannot
be easily identified, as can town planners. This is because there is no
comparable explicit theoretical statement of their views. Nor can there
be a clear discourse of how their various socio-political stances afford
varying support for the intended administrative and legitimatory
functions of health services planning. In any case, all three of the roles
which are evidenced in mainstream planning theory are inadequate for
an expression of my own socio-political view. What must be considered
here is the commonality of the three roles, a commonality which
embodies a socio-political acceptance of the productive aspects of
planning work. In health services planning, this includes the acceptance
of both the 'functional' definition of health and the specification of
particular health care resources as the 'object-resources' of planning
work. Individual health services planners may regard the distributive
purposes of their work differently and this may contribute to plans
for differently distributed health services. Yet, by accepting the
'object-resources' of planning action, these planners demonstrate a
common socio-political neutrality to *what* health services planners
plan and, consequently, to the legitimatory and administrative
functions which are fulfilled as a result. This is not demonstrated in a
body of comparative theory, as in town planning, but it is apparent in
what the health services planner *does* to plan.

The operational activities of planning action are based on an
assumption of the scientific objectivity of medicine. Despite seeming
changes in the health services planning process to include setting
objectives and targets, despite the fact that the actual allocation of manpower, money and buildings is a late step in the planning process,
health services are still prescribed as resource packages of medical and
non-medical treatment which the population needs. Causes of ill-health,
priorities of medical treatment, prescriptions of new service are all

outside the scope of planning action. Planning alternatives take the form of the 'deployment of resources so as to give the best choice between various possible methods of delivery of treatment' (Dunnell and Holland, 1973, p. 256). Planners deal with 'delivery'; but 'treatment' is the key word for required services, and only the physician prescribes treatment.

> In technical arguments [regarding medicine] one expects to reach mutually acceptable answers, and the reason for this is that it is assumed in such arguments that, given the publicly known parameters of the case, there is one best way to maximize whatever value is to be maximized. (Fay, 1975, p. 22.)

The one best way, as Renaud (1975) has argued, is based on the 'engineering model of modern scientific medicine', a model derived from the functional conception of health. Within the 'model', health services are specified and ranked to maximise the improvement of the economic and social conditions required for capital accumulation.

Now, physiologically, certain health services may indeed be more effective and efficient than others in treating certain ailments. However, it is the relative priority of each service within a given range of health care resources which takes on the label of 'the best way'. 'Medical strategy' becomes the accepted, correct, scientific way of grouping and providing specified quantities and packages of health services, purportedly devoid of any political and economic influences. But despite the fact that the very intervention of the state 'automatically politicizes health care delivery' (p. 566), the action space of planning work is accepted as apolitical and the planner's role is to deal with it 'apolitically'.

Thus, the health services planning process is a means for allocating the resources which are required by the needs of capital to accommodate the range of acceptable health services. This process can take the form of non-technical planning discussions based on a common 'medico-image' of what the given range of health services is. It can also take the form of a systematic and technical planning methodology, wherein the given services are identified for each resource package. And there are other forms and other approaches of what planners do to plan. The point is this: the health services planner accepts the given range of health services as a *neutral corpus* of planning work and, by doing so, the planner undertakes the work as a neutral technician, even though considerations of 'accessibility' or 'acceptance-of-the-population' may be argued to interject political value.

Goal-setting, plan formulation, plan evaluation all follow. The techniques which are undertaken to operationalise these planning steps may, in themselves, reflect various socio-political stances (see Rosenhead, 1976a); they may further aid the concealment of the social and economic influences which determine the composition of community health services. But they do not question the administrative aspects of health services planning work. By remaining neutral to the action space of health services planning, planners collude — consciously or not — with the legitimatory activities of the capital-owning class. With health services given at any one time, the health services planner, as with planners of other disciplines, deals only with the distributional aspects of health services planning work: organisation and distribution of the resources and facilities which are required to accommodate prescribed services. Relationships to production and to the economic basis of society are ignored.

What Difference does it Make?

Planners can not, as individuals, alter the conditions of their work. The dimensions of planning work — action space, operational activities and the planner's role — are all influenced, to varying degrees, by the social conditions within which planners work. And even if some planners' socio-political views influence the adoption of planning roles contrary to that which is expected by the state employer, those planners are still faced with a definition of planning problems and a process of planning work which is largely outside their control. They still have to work within an institution and with other planners who adhere to opposing political views. And, in the end, planners still have to work.

If this is the end, why go through the effort of understanding the real conditions of work and political-economic structure of society at all? Why think 'differently'? If the planner's work contributes to the capital-owning class's interests irrespective of individual socio-political views, why bother worrying about it?

The point is this: an awareness of the real class conflicts which underlie the structure of society and the conditions of all work and production activities which take place within it is not the end at all. It is the beginning.

Within the planning workplace there is little opportunity for the planner to directly manifest this awareness. Where there is some latitude for socio-political expression, the planner may base individual actions upon the types of questions which Rosenhead (1976b) proposes for others. Does the work increase exploitation? Does it increase 'mystification' of the real organisation of society? In my view, the answer for the health services planner is often 'yes', and this involves making choices about which side of the social struggle the planner is on. But taking sides on issues which the planner sees as related to 'control or co-optation of conflict' must be weighed against the occupational risks which the planner takes in acting against the interest of the state employer. Sometimes the risks may be worth it; at other times, they may not. In many cases, the choice will not be available.

But the real importance of comprehending the social conditions of one's work lies in knowing that the choice exists. It lies in becoming aware that work and the individual who undertakes it are social elements interrelated within social structure with all other individuals in shared or conflicting interests. The role of the planner who plans health services (or towns or roadways) becomes one which recognises the ineffectiveness of individual action. The planner is not an individual agent of change. The planner realises that by working as if the individual can make a difference, he or she is likely to support only the legitimatory function of the state, and to lend further strength to the power of the capital-owning class.

I believe that the struggle for individual existence must disappear.[4] This does not mean that the struggle to live or to learn must end; what it does mean is that the attitude in which the individual is seen as the basis for social organisation must end. The individual planner becomes conscious of his or her social existence. Thus the planner takes on the role of imparting a knowledge of the conditions of social organisation to other oppressed individuals with whom the planner lives and works. Where choices can be made, real conflicts can be exposed. And there are many ways in which the planner can do this: by arguing knowledgably against the functional nature of health, by questioning the legitimatory practices of government health agencies, by using the process of planning to enlighten others to attempts to abolish political debate in planning, by questioning the resource packages which accommodate health services, by asking, 'who profits from planners' work?'. This is how the planner who is enlightened to the social conditions of planning work must plan: by exposing to *social* struggle the conflicts which state planning means to conceal.

I will spend the remainder of this book looking at one of the more important of these issues, the confrontation between planners and physicians. Given the nature of planning work, questions regarding

distribution of health care resources are legitimately open to the health
services planner. Naturally, debates — relatively harmless to the
interests of capital — arise over how these resources and the services
which they accommodate should be distributed. And these debates
often embroil the planner in the arguments between providers and
users of health services. After all, it is the providers of services —
that is, physicians — who lend the authoritative professional weight
to prescriptions of acceptable health services. Planners argue with
physicians over how services are to be provided and, more frequently,
over who is to decide (see, for example, Klarman, 1976, and Frieden
and Peters, 1970). These arguments enlarge a conflict which I believe
aids the avoidance and diffusion of the class conflicts which would
directly challenge the power of capital.

This is an important debate in health services planning. It has
direct effects on the planner's role and, as such, it merits close
examination.

Physicians versus Planners

Chapter 3, in part, reviewed the current and growing debate about the
medical profession's control over 'health'. Because it holds 'professional
jurisdiction' — as Friedson terms it — over the health field generally,
the medical profession represents the most apparent collective interest
in health services planning. However, challengers have arisen to question
the traditional, scientific and clinical grounds upon which the medical
profession has founded its seemingly absolute control over health and
health services. And these challengers include some who are medical
professionals themselves.

Obviously, the collective interest of the medical profession is not
delineated inclusively or solely on professional lines. The confrontation
which Mahler described between the 'medical Establishment' and the
'people outside' is not so much a battle between individuals in and
out of the medical profession as an apparent conflict between what
Robert Alford (1975) has called the 'structural interests' in 'health
care politics'.

Alford's book *Health Care Politics* is an important contribution to
the knowledge of the political influences upon health services provision
and planning. As such, it serves as a good explanation of the provider-
user debate in which health services planners find themselves em-
broiled. The study which Alford documents demonstrates a commonly-
voiced theory of 'ideological and interest group barriers' to health care
reform. Underlying these barriers is the relative power enjoyed by what

Alford identifies as structural interests.

> These are interests which are more than potential interest groups . . .
> which are merely waiting for the opportunity or the necessity of
> organizing to present demands or grievances to the appropriate
> authorities. Rather, structural interests either do not have to be
> organized in order to have their interests served or cannot be
> organized without great difficulty. (p. 14.)

Alford describes three structural interests operating in the provision
of health care, and he classifies them as *dominant*, *challenging* and
repressed.

The Concept of Competing Interest Groups

The dominant structural interest is presented by the 'professional
monopolists'. Alford includes in this group not only medical
practitioners but also bio-medical researchers, all of whom, through
their professional associations, are able to exercise 'nearly complete
control over the conditions of their work' (p. 194). Although the
terminology which Alford employs in defining the 'dominant'
classification is similar to that in Johnson's collegiate control definition,
Alford's concept emphasises a more limited area of occupational
jurisdiction. The dominant structural interest is concerned primarily
with control over health care resources, the distribution and cost of
medical services, the supply of physicians, the monopoly of legally
sanctioned skills and knowledge required for medical diagnosis and
treatment — all matters subscribed within the planner's action space,
though many not open to question.

The challenging structural interest seeks to break 'the professional
monopoly of physicians over the production and distribution of
health care' (p. 15). Alford calls this interest 'corporate rationalization'
and groups together health administrators, medical schools, government
health planners, public health agencies and researchers and others as a
rather unorganised interest body. 'Their ideology stresses a rational,
efficient, cost-conscious, coordinated health care delivery system'
(p. 204). As a result they rely heavily on 'coordination, integration,
and planning' in the hope of bringing medical care providers under the
umbrella of bureaucratic control. Again, this could be explained in
Johnson's vocabulary as imposing mediative control upon the
medical profession. But, Alford notes that the inability of corporate
rationalisers to control all of the factors of health production, for a

myriad of reasons — not least of which is the monopolisers dominant structural power — leads 'to failures of planning and coordination in practice'.

The repressed structural interest is that of the 'community population' who find their spokesmen in 'equal-health advocates'. Here Alford would include many of the critics of 'medicine as health', including those who may also be physicians, although these latter individuals, Alford suggests, would be 'academic', not 'practicing', physicians. However, Alford claims that, for the most part, the activities of equal-health advocates either legitimise the interests of professional monopolists (when the activities are directed against particular programmes, for example) or legitimise the interests of corporate rationalisers (when, for example, the activities focus on reorganisation of the health system). It is only to the extent that equal-health advocates 'can create consciousness among the community population' of the causes of ineffective and inefficient health care that Alford sees the groundwork being laid 'for a more fundamental challenge to the powers of the major structural interests' (p. 220).

Alford sees the three structural interests in conflict over the control of the provision of medical and other health services at the point of consumption — that is, over 'health care delivery'. However, conflicts between the structural interests are not restricted to health care delivery. Indeed, Alford points out that medical professionals, who dominate the professional monopolist interest, have extended their monopoly power throughout the health field;[5] and here too the medical profession is being challenged. But it is in the delivery of health services where the conflict between structural interests is most apparent. Alford narrows in on the arguments between physicians and planners, arguing that the conflict between professional monopolists and corporate rationalisers is obstructing the achievement of effective and efficient health care sought by the equal-health advocates. However, in his view, it is the power exercised by professional monopolists which is the principal barrier.[6]

Others (e.g. Battistella, 1972 and Robson, 1973) have identified collective interests in health care delivery not dissimilar to those put forward by Alford. The numbers and labels of interest groups are not important. Basically, they break down into medical practitioners seeking to maintain self-control over the conditions of work, bureaucrats seeking to impose corporate planning control over health services and professionals, and consumers (led by 'democratic humanists') seeking 'good' health care. These classifications are not unimportant; they contribute towards an understanding of the mechanics of some of the current political debates which surround health and health services. But these structural interests are not the influences which dominantly affect health services planning, because their compositions largely ignore the fundamental class interests of capitalist society. As a result, the conflict between structural interests is one which ignores the nature of health and the nature of health services provision as defined by the needs of the capital-owning class.

Professional Power and Class Interest in Planning

Within the scope of health services planning, the conflict which Alford and others describe is one between medical practitioners and health bureaucrats. The structural interests of professional monopolists, on the one hand, and of corporate rationalisers, on the other, are engaged in a conflict over the control of health services provision. These two groups compete within the institutionalised health services planning activity to fill the *occupational* role of the health services planner. And this is what the health services planning conflict is really about. It is essentially a fight between a professionally *dominated* occupational group (professional monopolists) and a professionally *diverse* occupational group (corporate rationalisers). The competition between these occupational groups is a conflict over jurisdiction in health services provision: a 'false-conflict' over who plans and who decides how to provide health services, health services whose productive nature is predetermined. It is false, not because it does not exist but because it does not strike at the basis of real political-economic control in a capitalist society.

This 'false-conflict' tends to conceal the point that health services planning does not determine what health services are going to be provided and, by concealing this reality, aids the legitimatory practices of the state.[7] *What* planners plan, generally, and *what* health services planners plan, in particular, are dictated by the need for the state to fulfil its functions within capitalist society. These functions are dictated by the political-economic requirements of the dominant power holders in that society, the owners of capital. But what Alford calls the 'noisy debate' over health services provision, particularly as it focuses on the conflict over the health service planning occupation, becomes legitimised and then propagandised as real conflict over health services. In actuality, it is a conflict between agents of capital, which results in yet another benefit to the owners of capital. What conflicts do arise *appear* to be conflicts involving those who plan health services and those who provide health services. When used as the forum for the prevailing user-provider health debates, these false conflicts undermine the potential which social protest over health services may have had in strengthening the political power of the working class against the owners of capital. Instead of serving as part of the broader political-economic class struggle, social protests over health services, because they are channelled through the institutionalised and legitimised activities of the state, become a conflict between technocrats and bureaucrats, on the one hand, and health services consumers without capital-owning power, on the other.

This 'false-conflict' is evident in the attack on the 'bureaucratization of health' championed by Illich. In my view, this kind of protest is largely counter-productive to the realisation of the real interests of the working class. Its most insidious result is that it tends to further divide the working class in struggles within itself, like other forms of false-conflict (e.g., racism and sexism) which are surreptitiously promoted by the capital-owning class. The capital-owning class can withstand these social protest 'attacks' because, and so long as, they do not challenge their own interests.

By attacking professional monopolists, the corporate rationaliser planners are *not* attacking the interests of the capital-owning class. Nor, by attacking the other structural interests, are the 'equal-health advocates' attacking the interests of the capital-owning class *except insofar as those groups being attacked represent economically, or ideologically, capitalist interests.*

Now, this last emphasis is important, but it should not be over-stated. The *class* interests of the groups involved in considerations of health and health services can represent the real interests involved in society's class struggle. Johnson's discussion shows the importance of class associations of professional groups in establishing, maintaining and exercising their professional power. And the dominant professional power in the health field is the medical profession, whose 'social class' composition is determined largely by socialisation processes controlled by the capital-owning class.[8] Navarro's (1974b) discussion emphasises the need to understand this phenomenon as a determinant of professional power:

> Social class and income differentials come about because of the different degrees of ownership, control, and influence that different social classes have over the means of production and consumption

and over the organs of legitimization, including the media,
communications, education, and even the organs of the state. (p. 74.)

Robson's (1973) study in the UK and Berliner's (1975) study in the
US have shown that the professional power of the medical profession is
founded predominantly on the interests of capital (partially by birth)
and how that power operates to strengthen further and legitimise those
class interests.

When members of the medical profession collectively exercise their
professional power to control the conditions of their work, they are
acting similarly to other professional groups. However, insofar as the
class interest of the owners of capital is strengthened or protected from
conflict through the exercise of medical professional power, the
influence resulting from the conflict between the medical profession
and other professions over the health services planner occupation
is socially significant, because class political power has taken the form
of professional power.

The professional monopolists, or whatever other label is attributed
to the medical practitioner group, is regarded basically as a professional
group with collegiate professional power over the conditions of its
work. Corporate rationalisers, on the other hand, are a professionally
diverse group which includes medical professionals, planning professionals,
and others, all of whom, as members of different professional groups,
hold different levels of professional power. This point emphasises the
false nature of the conflict which Alford and others describe. The
conflict between the professionally powerful professional monopolists
and the occupational grouping of corporate rationalisers is either a
professional conflict or a conflict between a group which *is* capable
of exercising political-economic power and a group which is not
collectively organised on such a political-economic basis. Comparing
professional monopolists with corporate rationalisers in this latter
conflict situation — which is what the physician versus planner debate
and, more broadly, the user-provider debate do — is like comparing
heavyweight boxers with punching bags. There is not enough common
ground for a fight.

But an important question must be asked before discarding this
'false-conflict' altogether. What about the medical professionals in the
corporate rationalisation and in the community population interests?

Certainly individual medical professionals can display socio-political
interests which are not in line with those of the medical profession as
a whole, either because of the infrequently 'allowed' entry of working

class persons into the medical profession (see Robson, 1973) or
because of independent socio-political thought. But this does not mean
that all medical professionals categorised in corporate rationalisation or
other bureaucratic groups do *not* adhere to the interests of the medical
profession. These groupings are only occupational; medico members of
technocratic or bureaucratic occupations may share occupational
interests in 'co-ordination, integration and planning' while simultaneously sharing professional interests which reflect the interests of
the capital-owning class. The converse of this is also true. Medical
practitioners who may, in Alford-esque analysis, be grouped in the
professional monopolist interest do *not* necessarily adhere to the
profession's interests. Restating an earlier argument, people do not
think solely 'as physicians', nor 'as planners', nor 'as corporate
rationalisers', even though the professional affiliation and the
class requirements for professional entry may influence socio-political
thought to adhere to a collective, professional and class-based interest.

Medical professionals may be capitalists or may, using Navarro's
terms, have a 'degree of ownership' over the means of production
(presumably through market wealth). In this case the interests of the
capital-owning class are the real interests of those medical professionals.
However, in other individual cases they are not. This does not mean,
however, that all medical professionals consciously collaborate with or
support capitalist interests. There may be conscious commitment to
existing political and economic organisations in order to preserve the
financial and social benefits which they afford medical professionals.
But such support may well be gained, by the capital-owning class,
through its own legitimatory activities. Physicians, too, can suffer
from false-consciousness.

With all of this said, the apparent interest groupings which Alford
and others have studied can not be ignored. They do present an image
of conflict within the health services planning workplace. Physicians,
on the one hand, and bureaucrats of many professions, on the other,
do confront each other, collectively, in debate and political manoeuvre
over who will control the planning of health services provision and
over the advantages and disadvantages afforded by the planning
approach of each. The importance of this conflict, however, lies not
in its affecting the work of the health services planners but in
furthering the legitimatory activities of the capital-owning class by
making latent real social conflict.

The health services planner, therefore, must reject the notion of a
conflict between 'structural interests' such as those put forward by

Alford. The conflict between professional and occupational interests in the health services planning workplace is an activity which arises *from* the needs of late capitalist society, and, as such, only serves as a *medium* by which the social organisation of capital further influences planning action. The role of the planner is to understand this type of influence.

A Continuing Thought

It is not the consciousness of men that determines their existence, but their social existence determines their consciousness. (Marx, 1970b, p. 21.)

With the exposure of the capital-owning class's real interests and with the spread of the social understanding of work, the working class gains its strength and takes on the continued role of conflict with the owners of capital. And for the health services planner this is where conflict is fought − on a class basis, not as an individual 'liberalising' planner.

The movement towards understanding the social conditions of life and work require patient and continuing education. It requires a continuous challenge to the shadow of legitimisation which the capital-owning class casts over the conditions of work and the conditions of social organisation.

For the planner, this begins with the realisation that planning is both an occupation and an idea. (Parston, 1980, p. 23.)

Notes

1. See Chapter 1.
2. See Conover (1973) for an analysis of social class and chronic illness. Friedman (1974) cites Hames's Evans County, Georgia study which relates 'socio-economic status' to incidence of coronary heart disease.
3. *Patient Care Classification by Types of Care*, a publication of the Ontario Ministry of Health (1975), is a fine example of this prescription of resources, translating 'care' into 'chronic hospitals', 'public hospitals', 'psycho-geriatric units', etc.
4. 'With the seizing of the means of production by society . . . the struggle for individual existence disappears.' (Engels, 1974, p. 76.)
5. Alford explains the extent of this monopoly:

Physicians have extracted an arbitrary subset from the array of skills and knowledge relevant to the maintenance of health in a population, have successfully defined these as their property to be sold for a price, and have managed to create legal mechanisms which enforce that monopoly and social beliefs which have mystified the population about the appropriateness and desirability of that monopoly. (p. 195.)

6. It is difficult to separate professional power from a consideration of Alford's case, especially because of the multi-professional composition of his structural interests. Members of the medical profession, who enjoy collegiate control over their conditions of work, predominantly compose the 'professional monopolist' interests. Nevertheless, *some* medical professionals (all of whom, in Alford's groupings, are likely to be non-practitioners) do number among the corporate rationalisers and equal-health advocates. Alford recognises that professional affiliation by training neither *ensures* adherence to a professional structural interest nor does it mean that one's occupation will follow one's profession, particularly in the case of the medical professional.

7. Alford sees the contribution of this 'conflict' to the state's legitimatory function in this way:

Noisy debate conceals unity of commitment to working through existing political challenges, which may account for the unwillingness of the bureaucratic reformers — visibly more dissatisfied with the organization of health care — to mobilize potential allies with the rhetoric and political tactics which could generate an effective movement for change. (p. 253.)

8. Professional planners, who do not share the same professional power as professional medicos, are largely 'drawn' from sociological classes of a wider range and of generally lower status than medical professionals (see Marcus, 1971).

REFERENCES

Abel-Smith, B. (1964), *The Hospital 1800–1948*, London: Heinemann
Educational Books Ltd
—— (1976), *Value for Money in Health Services*, London: Heinemann
Educational Books Ltd
Abel-Smith, B. and Titmuss, R. (1956), *The Cost of the National Health
Service in England and Wales*, London: Cambridge University Press
Abercrombie, P. (1945), *Greater London Plan 1944*, London: HMSO
Ackoff, R.L. (1974a), *Redesigning the Future*, New York: John Wiley
& Sons
—— (1974b), 'The Social Responsibility of Operational Research',
Operational Research Quarterly, vol. 25, pp. 361–71
—— (1975), 'A Reply to the Comments of Chesterton, Goodsman,
Rosenhead and Thunhurst', *Operational Research Quarterly*, vol. 26,
pp. 96–9
—— (1976), 'Does Quality of Life have to be Quantified?', *Operational
Research Quarterly*, vol. 27, pp. 289–303
Albury-Wodonga Development Corporation (1976), *Health Services for
a New City: A Guide for Action*, Report of the Albury-Wodonga
Health Study Team, Albury, New South Wales
Alford, R.R. (1975), *Health Care Politics*, Chicago: University of
Chicago Press
Altshuler, A. (1965), 'The Goals of Comprehensive Planning', *JAIP*,
vol. 31, pp. 186–95
Anderson, N.N. and Robins, L. (1976), 'Observations on Potential
Contributions of Health Planning', *IJHS*, vol. 6, pp. 651–66
Andrieux, A. and Lignon, J. (1960), *L'Ouvrier d'aujourd'hui*, Paris:
Marcel Rivière
Atkinson, D. (1971), *Orthodox Consensus and Radical Alternative: A
Study in Sociological Theory*, London: Heinemann Educational
Books Ltd
Australia (1974), *A Report on Hospitals in Australia*, Hospital and
Health Services Commission, Canberra: Australian Government
Publishing Service
Axelrod, S.J., Donabedian, A. and Gentry, D.W. (1976), *Medical Care
Chart Book*, Sixth Edition, Ann Arbor: University of Michigan
Bachrach, P. and Baratz, M.S. (1962), 'The Two Faces of Power' in

Castle *et al.* (eds.), *Decisions, Organizations and Society*, Middlesex: Penguin Books Ltd

Banfield, E.C. (1959), 'Ends and Means in Planning' in Faludi, A. (ed.), *A Reader in Planning Theory*, Oxford: Pergamon Press Ltd, 1973

Battistella, R.M. (1972), 'Rationalization of Health Services: Political and Social Assumptions', *IJHS*, vol. 2, pp. 331–48

Beck, R.G. (1973), 'Economic Class and Access to Physician Services under Public Medical Insurance', *IJHS*, vol. 3, pp. 341–55

Beckman, N. (1964), 'The Planner as Bureaucrat', *JAIP*, vol. 30, pp. 323–7

Bennett, J.E. and Krasney, J. (1977), 'Health-Care in Canada', reprinted from the series appearing in *The Financial Post*, Toronto, 26 March–7 May

Bennis, W.G., Benne, K.D. and Chin, R. (eds.) (1969), *The Planning of Change: Readings in Applied Behavioral Sciences*, New York: Holt, Rinehart and Winston

Berliner, H.S. (1975), 'A Larger Perspective on the Flexner Report', *IJHS*, vol. 5, pp. 573–92

Bispham, K., Thorne, S. and Holland, W.W. (1971), 'Information for Area Health Planning' in McLachlan, G. (ed.), *Challenges for Change: Essays on the Next Decade in the NHS*, London: Oxford University Press

Blum, H.L. (1974), *Planning for Health*, New York: Human Sciences Press

Bottomore, T. (1965), *Classes in Modern Society*, London: George Allen & Unwin Ltd

Boulding, K.E. (1967), 'The Concept of Need for Health Services' in Mainland, D. (ed.), *Health Services Research*, New York: Milbank Memorial Fund

Braverman, H. (1974), *Labor and Monopoly Capital*, New York: Monthly Review Press

Bridges-Webb, C. (1971), 'A Study of Mortality in Traralgon, Victoria', Melbourne: Monash University, MD Thesis

Bright, M. (1972). 'The Demographic Base for Health Planning' in Reinke, W.A. (ed.), *Health Planning*, Baltimore: Johns Hopkins Universit

Cassidy, M. (1971), 'Social Indicators' in *Official Architecture and Planning*, March, pp. 195–7

Castells, M. (1976), 'The Service Economy and Postindustrial Society: A Sociological Critique', *IJHS*, vol. 6, pp. 595–607

Castle, B. (1976), *NHS Revisited*, Fabian Tract 440, London: Fabian Society

Chapman, R.H., Coffey, R.J. and Peltzie, K.G. (1977), 'A Generic Process for Planning Health Services', *American Journal of Health Planning*, vol. 2, pp. 39–44

Chesterton, K., Goodsman, R., Rosenhead, J. and Thunhurst, C. (1975), 'A Comment on Ackoff's "The Social Responsibility of Operational Research" ', *Operational Research Quarterly*, vol. 26, pp. 91–5

Clapp, J.A. (1971), *New Towns and Urban Policy*, New York: Dunellen

Cochrane, A.L. (1972), *Effectiveness and Efficiency*, London: The Nuffield Provincial Hospitals Trust

Cockburn, C. (1977), *The Local State – Management of Cities and People*, London: Pluto Press

Conover, P.W. (1973), 'Social Class and Chronic Illness', *IJHS*, vol. 3, pp. 357–68

Cowan, P.D. (1969), 'Hospital Siting and Location in Relation to Urban Land Use and Development', London: University of London, PhD Thesis

—— (1971), 'Utopians, Scientists and Forecasters: Approaches to Understanding and City', paper presented to the Fourth International Congress on Man and Society, Herceg-Novi, Yugoslavia, July

—— (ed.) (1973), *The Future of Planning*, London: Heinemann Educational Books Ltd

—— (nd), 'Milton Keynes: A Discussion', unpublished paper

Cox, C. and Mead, A. (eds.) (1975), *A Sociology of Medical Practice*, London: Collier-Macmillan Publishers

Crossman, R. (1972), *A Politician's View of Health Services Planning*, Maurice B. Loch Lecture, Glasgow: University of Glasgow

Dahl, R.A. (1961), *Who Governs?*, New Haven: Yale University Press

Dahl, R.A. and Lindblom, C.E. (1953), *Politics, Economics and Welfare*, New York: Harper and Brothers

Davidoff, P. (1965), 'Advocacy and Pluralism in Planning', *JAIP*, vol. 31, pp. 331–8

Davidoff, P. and Reiner, T.A. (1962), 'A Choice Theory of Planning', *JAIP*, vol. 28, pp. 103–15

Davies, J.G. (1972), *The Evangelistic Bureaucrat: A Study of a Planning Exercise in Newcastle-upon-Tyne*, London: Tavistock

de Monchaux, J. and Milton Keynes Medical Planning Group (1969), 'Milton Keynes – A Joint Approach to Planning', *British Medical Journal*, March, pp. 628–32, reprint

Dennis, N. (1970), *People and Planning*, London: Faber and Faber

Dillane, J.B. (1966), 'General Practice in the New Towns of Britain', *Reports from General Practice*, no. 6, London: College of General

Practitioners

Dingle, J.H. (1973), 'The Ills of Man', in *Life and Death and Medicine*, A Scientific American Book, San Francisco: W.H. Freeman and Co.

Dobb, M. (1958), 'What is Capitalism?' in Melmerstein, D. (ed.), *Economics – Mainstream Readings and Radical Critiques*, New York: Random House (1973)

Dowie, J. (1975), 'The Portfolio Approach to Health Behaviour', *Social Science and Medicine*, vol. 8, pp. 619–31

Draper, P.A., Barnard, K., Dalgleish, P.G., Edgar, W., Gooding, D.G., Goodman, M. and Young, K.D. (1971), *Planning Health Services in New Communities: The Technical Problems*, Report of Working Group II, London: Department of Health and Social Security

Draper, P., Best, G. and Dennis, J. (1976), *Health, Money and the National Health Service*, London: Unit for the Study of Health Policy, Guy's Hospital Medical School

—— (1977), 'Health & Wealth', London: Unit for the Study of Health Policy, Guy's Hospital Medical School

Dror, Y. (1963), 'The Planning Process: A Facet Design' in Faludi, A. (ed.) (1973), *A Reader in Planning Theory*, Oxford: Pergamon Press Ltd

Dubos, R. (1959), *Mirage of Health: Utopias, Progress and Bioligical Change*, New York: Perennial Library, Harper & Row

Dummer, J. (1973), 'The Planning Function' in *Community Medicine*, The Hospital Centre Reprint No. 737, pp. 340–2

Dunnell, K. (ed.) (1976), *Health Services Planning*, London: King Edward's Hospital Fund

Dunnell, K. and Holland, W.W. (1973), 'Planning for Health Services' in *Annual Report*, St Thomas' Social Medicine and Health Services Research Unit, London: St Thomas' Hospital and Medical School

Dyckman, J.W. (1961), 'What Makes Planners Plan?', *JAIP*, vol. 27, pp. 164–7

Eckstein, H. (1959), *The English Health Services*, London: Oxford University Press

Eden, W.A. (1947), 'Ebenezer Howard and the Garden City Movement', *Town Planning Review*, vol. 19, pp. 123–43

Engels, F. (1968a), 'Introduction to Marx's *The Civil War in France*' in *Marx and Engels: Selected Works*, London: Lawrence and Wishart Ltd

—— (1968b), 'Introduction to Marx's *The Class Struggles in France*' in *Marx and Engels: Selected Works*, London: Lawrence and Wishart Ltd

Engels, F. (1968c), 'To J Bloch in Königsberg' in *Marx and Engels: Selected Works*, London: Lawrence and Wishart Ltd
—— (1974), *Socialism: Utopian and Scientific*, Moscow: Progress Publishers
Etzioni, A. (1967), 'Mixed-Scanning: A "Third" Approach to Decision-Making' in Faludi, A. (ed.) (1973), *A Reader in Planning Theory*, Oxford: Pergamon Press Ltd
Fagence, M. (1975), 'Town Planner as Diplomat — An Exploration of a Dimension of a Planner's Political Role', *Royal Australian Planning Institute Journal*, April, pp. 58—65
Falk, L.A. and Hawkins, J.N. (1975), 'Serve the People: What It Would Mean for Health Care in the United States' in Ingman, S.R. and Thomas, A.E. (eds.), *Topias and Utopias in Health*, The Hague: Mouton Publishers
Faludi, A. (ed.) (1973), *A Reader in Planning Theory*, Oxford: Pergamon Press Ltd
Fay, B. (1975), *Social Theory and Political Practice*, London: George Allen & Unwin Ltd
Feldstein, M.S. (1967), 'An Aggregate Planning Model of the Health Care Sector', *Medical Care*, vol. 5, pp. 369—81
—— (1973), 'The Medical Economy' in *Life and Death and Medicine*, A Scientific American Book, San Francisco: W.H. Freeman and Co.
Fisher, J.C. (1962), 'Planning the City of Socialist Man', *JAIP*, vol. 28, pp. 251—5
Florey, C. du V. and Weddell, J.M. (1976), 'The Epidemiologist's Contribution' in Dunnell, K. (ed.), *Health Services Planning*, London: King Edward's Hospital Fund
Forsyth, G. (1973), *Doctors and State Medicine*, Second Edition, Tunbridge Wells, Kent: Pitman Publishing Co. Ltd
Fox, J. (1973), 'Technological Components of Health Planning' in *Community Medicine*, The Hospital Centre Reprint No. 737, pp. 346—71
Frieden, B.J. and Peters, J. (1970), 'Urban Planning and Health Services: Opportunities for Cooperation', *AIPJ*, vol. 36, pp. 82—95
Friedman, G.D. (1974), *Primer of Epidemiology*, New York: McGraw-Hill Book Company
Friedmann, J. (1965), 'A Response to Altshuler', *JAIP*, vol. 31, pp. 195—7
Friedmann, J. and Hudson, B. (1974), 'Knowledge and Action: A Guide to Planning Theory', *AIPJ*, vol. 40, pp. 2—16
Friedson, E. (1970), *Profession of Medicine*, New York: Dodd, Mead

and Co.

Friend, J.K. and Jessop, W.N. (1969), *Local Government and Strategic Choice*, London: Tavistock Publications

Friend, J.K., Power, J.M. and Yewlett, C.J. (1974), *Public Planning: The Inter-Corporate Dimension*, London: Tavistock Publications

Fry, J. (1969), *Medicine in Three Societies*, Aylesbury, Bucks: MTP

Fry, J. and McKenzie, J. (1966), 'The Provision of General Medical Care in New Towns', Proceedings of a Symposium held at the College of General Practitioners, 19—20 April, London: Office of Health Economics

Fuchs, V.R. (1967), 'The Contribution of Health to the American Economy' in Mainland, D. (ed.), *Health Services Research*, New York: Milbank Memorial Fund

Galbraith, J.K. (1974), *The New Industrial State*, Middlesex: Penguin Books Ltd

Glass, R. (1959), 'The Evaluation of Planning: Some Sociological Considerations' in Faludi, A. (ed.) (1973), *A Reader in Planning Theory*, Oxford: Pergamon Press Ltd

Glazer, N. (1965), 'A Sociologist's View of Poverty' in Gordon, M.S. (ed.), *Poverty in America*, San Francisco: Chandler Publishing Co.

Godber, G. (1975), *The Health Service: Past, Present and Future*, London: University of London, The Athlone Press

Gooding, D.G. and Reid, J.J.A. (1970), 'Health Service Planning in New Towns', *The Medical Officer*, 3 April, pp. 177—80

Goodman, R. (1972), *After the Planners*, Middlesex: Penguin Books Ltd

Grabow, S. and Heskin, A. (1973), 'Foundations for a Radical Concept of Planning', *AIPJ*, vol. 39, pp. 106—14

Great Britain (1946), *Final Report of the New Towns Committee*, (The Reith Report), London: HMSO

—— (1964), *A Hospital Plan for England and Wales*, Ministry of Health, London: HMSO

—— (1965), *New Towns Act 1965*, Chapter 59, London: HMSO

—— (1969), *The Function of the District General Hospital*, (The Bonham-Carter Report), Department of Health and Social Security, Welsh Office, London: HMSO

—— (1972), *The New Towns of Britain*, Central Office of Information Reference Division, London: HMSO

Griffiths, D.A.T. (1971), 'Inequalities and Management in the NHS' in *The Hospital*, reprint

Gutch, R. (1970), 'Planning, philosophy and logic', *Journal of the*

Town Planning Institute, vol. 56, pp. 389—91

Habermas, J. (1973), 'Problems of Legitimation in Late Capitalism' in
Connerton, P. (ed.), *Critical Sociology*, Middlesex: Penguin Books
Ltd

—— (1974), *Theory and Practice*, London: Heinemann Educational
Books Ltd

Hall, P. (1972), 'Planning and the Environment' in Townsend and
Bosanquet (eds.), *Labour and Inequality*, London: The Fabian
Society

—— (1975), *Urban and Regional Planning*, Middlesex: Pelican
Books

Handler, A.B. (1957), 'What is Planning Theory?', *JAIP*, vol. 23,
pp. 144—50

Hart, J.T. (1971a), 'The Inverse Care Law', *Lancet*, I, pp. 405—12

—— (1971b), 'The National Health Service in England and Wales —
A Marxist Evaluation', Parts 1 and 2, *Marxism Today*, November and
December, pp. 327—32, 368—75

Harvey, D. (1973), *Social Justice and the City*, London: Edward
Arnold Ltd

Healy, P. (1974), 'The Problem of Ideology', *Journal of the Town
Planning Institute*, vol. 60, pp. 602—4

Hetzel, B.S. (1974), *Health and Australian Society*, Ringwood, Victoria:
Penguin Books Australia Ltd

Howard, E. (1945), Osborn, F.S. (ed.), *Garden Cities of To-Morrow*,
London: Faber & Faber Ltd

Illich, I. (1975), *Medical Nemesis — The Expropriation of Health*,
London: Calder and Boyars Ltd

Jackson, J.N. (1972), *The Urban Future*, London: George Allen &
Unwin Ltd

Jewkes, J. and Jewkes, S. (1961), *The Genesis of the British National
Health Service*, Oxford: Basil Blackwell

Johnson, T.J. (1972), *Professions and Power*, London: Macmillan

Kelman, S. (1975), 'The Social Nature of the Definition Problem in
Health', *IJHS*, vol. 5, pp. 625—42

Kennedy, E.M. (1972), *In Critical Condition — The Crisis in
America's Health Care*, New York: Simon and Schuster

Klarman, H.E. (1976), 'National Policies and Local Planning for Health
Services', *The Milbank Memorial Fund Quarterly*, vol. 54, pp. 1—28

Klein, R. (1972), 'The Political Economy of National Health', *The
Public Interest*, vol. 26, pp. 112—25

Knowles, J.H. (1973), 'The Hospital' in *Life and Death and Medicine*,

A Scientific American Book, San Francisco: W.H. Freeman and Co.

Knox, J.J. (1975), 'Democracy and Resistance to Change in Health Care', background paper for presentation at the Ciba Foundation, London, 9 December, mimeo

Krause, E.A. (1977), *Power and Illness*, New York: Elsevier North-Holland, Inc.

Krupinski, J., Stoller, A., Baikie, A.G. and Graves, J.E. (1970), *A Community Health Survey of the Rural Town of Heyfield Victoria, Australia*, Melbourne: Mental Health Authority Special Publication No. 1

Krupinski, J. and Stoller, A. (1971), *The Health of a Metropolis*, South Yarra, Victoria: Heinemann Educational Australia Pty Ltd

Laing, R.D. (1967), *The Politics of Experience*, Middlesex: Penguin Books Ltd

Lalonde, M. (1974), *A New Perspective on the Health of Canadians*, Ottawa: Information Canada

Letelier, O. (1976), 'The Chicago Boys in Chile', *The Review of Radical Political Economics*, vol. 8, no. 3, pp. 44–52

Levitt, R. (1976), *The Reorganized National Health Service*, London: Croom Helm

Lindblom, C.E. (1959), 'The Science of "Muddling Through" ' in Faludi, A. (ed.) (1973), *A Reader in Planning Theory*, Oxford: Pergamon Press Ltd

Lindsey, A. (1962), *Socialized Medicine in England and Wales*, Chapel Hill: The University of North Carolina Press

Lippitt, R.,Watson, J. and Westley, B. (1958), *The Dynamics of Planned Change*, New York: Harcourt, Brace and World

Ljobo, I. (1949), 'O Urbanistickoj Metodi', *Urbanizam Architektura*, vol. 25–7

Llewelyn-Davies, R. (1970), 'Milton Keynes – The Goals of the Plan', *The Royal Institute of British Architects Journal*, vol. 77, pp. 309–10

Logan, R.F.L. (1971), 'National Health Planning – An Appraisal of the State of the Art', *IJHS*, vol, 1, pp. 6–17

Logan, R.F.L., Ashley, J.S.A., Klein, R.E. and Robson, D.M. (1972), *Dynamics of Medical Care*, Memoir No. 14, London: London School of Hygiene and Tropical Medicine

Lukes, S. (1974), *Power – A Radical View*, Tiptree, Essex: The Anchor Press Ltd

McCallum, J.D. (1974), 'Planning Theory in Planning Education', *Journal of the Town Planning Institute*, vol. 60, pp. 738–41

MacEwen, M. (1970), 'Milton Keynes – ville bourgeoise', *The Royal*

Institute of British Architects Journal, vol. 77, pp. 315–6

McKeown, T. (1965), *Medicine in Modern Society*, London: George Allen & Unwin Ltd

—— (1976), 'A Background of Health Care Planning' in Kent, P.W. (ed.), *International Aspects of the Provision of Medical Care*, Stocksfield, Northumberland: Oriel Press Ltd

McKeown, T. and Lowe, C.R. (1966), *An Introduction to Social Medicine*, Oxford: Blackwell Scientific Publications

McKinlay, J.B. (1977), 'On the Medical-Industrial Complex', *American Medical News*, 11 April

McLoughlin, J.B. (1970), *Urban and Regional Planning: A Systems Approach*, London: Faber & Faber

Mahler, H. (1975), 'Health – A Demystification of Medical Technology', *Lancet*, vol. 2, no. 7940, pp. 829–33

Mandel, E. (1975), *Late Capitalism*, London: New Left Books

Mannheim, K. (1968), *Ideology and Utopia*, New York: Harcourt, Brace and World

Marcus, S.T. (1971), 'Planners – Who Are You?', *Journal of the Royal Institute of Town Planners*, vol. 57, pp. 54–9

Marx, K. (1968), 'Wage Labour and Capital' in *Marx and Engels: Selected Works*, London: Lawrence and Wishart Ltd

—— (1970a), *Capital*, vol. 1, London: Lawrence and Wishart Ltd

—— (1970b), *A Contribution to the Critique of Political Economy*, Moscow: Progress Publishers

—— (1973), *Grundrisse*, Middlesex: Penguin Books Ltd

Marx, K. and Engels, F. (1968), 'Manifesto of the Communist Party' in *Marx and Engels: Selected Works*, London: Lawrence and Wishart Ltd

—— (1974), *The German Ideology*, London: Lawrence and Wishart Ltd

Massey, D. (1974), 'Social Justice and the City: A Review', *Environment and Planning*, vol. 6, pp. 229–35

Maynard, A. (1975), *Health Care in the European Community*, London: Croom Helm

Mazziotti, D.F. (1974), 'The Underlying Assumptions of Advocacy Planning: Pluralism and Reform', *AIPJ*, vol. 40, pp. 38–47

Medawar, P.B. (1969), *Induction and Intuition in Scientific Thought*, London: Methuene & Co. Ltd

Medical Planning Group (1968a), Milton Keynes: *The Early Stage of Health Service Planning*, Not for Publication

—— (1968b), *A Health Service for Milton Keynes*, Department of

Health and Welfare, County Offices, Aylesbury, Bucks

Meyerson, M. (1956), 'Building the Middle-range Bridge for Comprehensive Planning' in Faludi, A. (ed.) (1973), *A Reader in Planning Theory*, Oxford: Pergamon Press Ltd

Meyerson, M. and Banfield, E.C. (1955), *Politics, Planning and the Public Interest*, Glencoe, Illinois: The Free Press

Milio, N. (1967), 'Values, Social Class and Community Health Services' in Cox, C. and Mead, A. (eds.), *A Sociology of Medical Practice*, London: Collier-Macmillan Publishers

Milton Keynes Development Corporation (1970), *The Plan for Milton Keynes*, vol. 1, prepared by Llewelyn-Davies Weeks Forestier-Walker and Bor, London

Milton Keynes Heath Service (1969), *Health Services Working Papers*, Buckinghamshire Area Health Authority

——— (1974), *Health Services Working Papers 1971–1973*, Buckinghamshire Area Health Authority

Myrdal, G. (1962), *Value in Social Theory*, London: Routledge & Kegan Paul Ltd

Navarro, V. (1974a), 'A Critique of the Present and Proposed Strategies for Redistributing Resources in the Health Sector and a Discussion of Alternatives', *Medical Care*, vol. 12, pp. 721–42

——— (1974b), 'The Political Economy of Medical Care: An Explanation of the Composition, Nature and Functions of the Present Health Sector of the United States', *IJHS*, vol. 5, pp. 65–94

——— (1975), 'The Industrialization of Fetishism or the Fetishism of Industrialization: A Critique of Ivan Illich', *IJHS*, vol. 5, pp. 351–71

——— (1976), *Medicine Under Capitalism*, London: Croom Helm and New York: Prodist

O'Connor, J. (1973), *The Fiscal Crisis of the State*, New York: St Martin's Press Inc.

OHE – Office of Health Economics (1974), *The Work of Primary Medical Care*, London: OHE

Ontario Ministry of Health (1975), *Patient Care Classifications by Types of Care*, Toronto: OMOH

Osborn, F.J. and Whittick, A. (1963), *The New Towns*, London: Lenard Hill

Owen, D. (1976), *In Sickness and Health: The Politics of Medicine*, London: Quartet Books Ltd

Peattie, L.R. (1968), 'Reflections on advocacy planning', *JAIP*, vol. 34, pp. 80–8

Peterson, W. (1966), 'On Some Meanings of "Planning" ', *JAIP*, vol. 32, pp. 130–42

Phelps-Brown, E.H. (1959), 'The Conditions of Work' in Potter and Sarre (eds.) (1974), *Dimensions of Society*, London: University of London Press Ltd

Piaget, J. (1971), *Structuralism*, London: Routledge & Kegan Paul Ltd

Piven, F.F. (1975), 'Planning and Class Interest', *AIPJ*, vol. 41, pp. 308–10

Postman, N. and Weingartner, C. (1971), *Teaching as a Subversive Activity*, Middlesex: Penguin Books Ltd

Poulantzas, N.A. (1975), *Political Power and Social Class*, London: New Left Books

Powell, J.E. (1976), *Medicine and Politics: 1975 and After*, Tunbridge Wells, Kent: Pitman Medical Publishing Co. Ltd

Powles, J. (1973), 'On the Limitations of Modern Medicine', *Medicine in Man*, vol. 1, pp. 1–30

Rabinovitz, F.F. (1967), 'Politics, Personality and Planning' in Faludi, A. (ed.) (1973), *A Reader in Planning Theory*, Oxford: Pergamon Press Ltd

Rapkin, C. and Ponte, R.W. (1975), 'The Decision Process in Urban Development: The Interaction of Planning and Politics in the United States and in the Less Developed Countries', *International Technical Cooperation Centre Review*, vol. 4

Read, M. (1966), *Culture, Health and Disease*, London: Tavistock Publications

Reid, J.J.A. and Gooding, D.G. (1975), 'Health Services Planning in a British New Town', *IJHS*, vol. 5, pp. 429–39

Reinke, W.A. (1972), 'An Overview of the Planning Process', in Reinke (ed.), *Health Planning*, Baltimore: Johns Hopkins University

Renaud, M. (1975), 'On the Structural Constraints to State Intervention in Health', *IJHS*, vol. 5, pp. 559–72

Ribicoff, A. (1972), *The American Medical Machine*, New York: Saturday Review Press

Risley, M. (1962), *The House of Healing: The Story of the Hospital*, London: Robert Hale Ltd

Robinson, I.M. (1972), *Decision-Making in Urban Planning*, Beverly Hills, California: Sage Publications

Robinson, J. and Eatwell, J. (1973), *An Introduction to Modern Economics*, London: McGraw-Hill

Robson, J. (1973), 'The NHS Company, Inc? — The Social Consequences

of the Professional Dominance in the National Health Service',
IJHS, vol. 3, pp. 413–26

Rodwin, L. (1956), *The British New Towns Policy*, Cambridge,
Massachusetts: Harvard University Press

Rondinelli, D.A. (1973), 'Urban Planning as Policy Analysis:
Management of Urban Change', *AIPJ*, vol. 39, pp. 13–22

Rose, E.A. (1974), 'Philosophy and Purpose of Planning' in Bruton
(ed.), *The Spirit and Purpose of Planning*, London: Hutchinson
and Co. Ltd

Rosenhead, J.V. (1976a), 'Operational Research in Urban and Social
Planning', paper prepared for the Second International Research
Conference on Operational Research, University of Sussex, April
—— (1976b), 'Some Further Comments on the Social
Responsibility of Operational Research', *Operational Research
Quarterly*, vol. 27, pp. 266–72

Rossdale, M. (1965), 'Health in a sick society', *New Left Review*, vol.
34, pp. 82–91

Russell, L.B. and Burke, C.S. (1978), 'The Political Economy of
Federal Health Programs in the United States: An Historical Review',
IJHS, vol. 8, pp. 55–77

Salkever, D.S. (1975), 'Economic Class and Differential Access to Care:
Comparisons among Health Care Systems', *IJHS*, vol. 5, pp. 373–95

Salmon, J.W. (1977), 'Monopoly Capital and the Reorganization of the
Health Sector', *The Review of Radical Political Economics*, vol. 9,
no. 1, pp. 125–33

Sax, S. (1972), *Medical Care in the Melting Pot*, Sydney: Angus and
Robertson Publishers Pty Ltd

Seely, J.R. (1962), 'What is Planning? Definition and Strategy', *JAIP*,
vol. 28

Sherrard, I.D. (ed.) (1968), *Social Welfare and Urban Problems*, New
York

Sichel, G.R.M. (1969), 'Planning of Health Services in New Towns' in
three parts in *Health Trends*, vol. 1, nos. 2 and 3; vol. 2, no. 2

Sigmond, R.M. (1967), 'Health Planning', *The Milbank Memorial Fund
Quarterly*, vol. 46, pp. 91–117

Simmie, J.M. (1974), *Citizens in Conflict*, London: Hutchinson
Educational Ltd

Soderstrom, L. (1978), *The Canadian Health System*, London: Croom
Helm Ltd

Stebbins, E.L. and Williams, K. (1972), 'History and Background of
Health Planning in the United States' in Reinke, W.A. (ed.), *Health*

Planning, Baltimore: Johns Hopkins University

Stewart, M. (1973), 'Markets, Choice and Urban Planning', *Town Planning Review*, vol. 44, pp. 203–20

Sweezy, P.M. (1970), *The Theory of Capitalist Development*, New York: Monthly Review Press

Taylor, C.E. (1972), 'Stages in the Planning Process' in Reinke, W.A. (ed.), *Health Planning*, Baltimore: Johns Hopkins University

Underwood, J. (1976), 'Structural Explanations of Planners' Use of Theory in Practice', paper for discussion at Central London Polytechnic, 20 November, mimeo

United States of America (1975), *Public Law 93–641*, (National Health Planning and Resources Development Act of 1974), 4 January
—— (1978), 'The US Health Service – HR 11879', *Congressional Record*, vol. 124, no. 47

Varlaam, A., Dragoumis, M. and Jefferys, M. (1972), 'Patients' Opinions of their Doctors', *Journal of the Royal College of General Practitioners*, vol. 22, p. 811

Venediktov, D.D. (1976), 'Some Problems of International Cooperation' in Kent, P.W. (ed.), *International Aspects of the Provision of Medical Care*, Stockfield, Northumberland: Oriel Press Ltd

Walker, R.A. (1950), *The Planning Function in Urban Government*, Second Edition, Chicago: University of Chicago Press

Warren, R.L. (1969), 'Model cities first round: Politics, planning and participation', *JAIP*, vol. 35, pp. 245–52

Webber, M.M. (1963), 'Comprehensive Planning and Social Responsibility: Toward an AIP Consensus on the Profession's Roles and Purposes', *JAIP*, vol. 29, pp. 232–41
—— (1968–9), 'Planning in an Environment of Change', *Town Planning Review*, vol. 39, pp. 179–95, 277–95

Wilson, A. (1973), 'How Planning Can Respond to New Issues' in Cowan, P.D. (ed.), *The Future of Planning*, London: Heinemann Educational Books Ltd

WHO – World Health Organisation (1972), *Health Hazards of the Human Environment*, Geneva: WHO
—— (1975), *Promoting Health in the Human Environment*, Geneva: WHO

Yamamoto, M. and Ohmura, J. (1975), 'The Health and Medical System in Japan', *Inquiry* (Chicago), vol. 12, no. 2, pp. 42–50

Zola, I.K. (1971), 'Medicine as an Institution of Social Control', in Cox, C. and Mead, A. (eds.), *A Sociology of Medical Practice*, London: Collier-Macmillan, 1975

Abbreviations in References

AIPJ/JAIP   −   *American Institute of Planners Journal/Journal of the American Institute of Planners*
IJHS   −   *International Journal of Health Services*

GENERAL INDEX

The letter-by-letter system has been adopted in both this and the author index. The aims of the book are set out under 'study'. Medical staff are dealt with under that entry and all health matters under 'health'.

191

AUTHOR INDEX